I BELONG

Biblical Reflections on Statelessness

Edited by Semegnish Asfaw

**World Council
of Churches**
Publications

I BELONG
Biblical Reflections on Statelessness
Edited by Semegnish Asfaw

WCC Publications is the book publishing programme of the World Council of Churches. Founded in 1948, the WCC promotes Christian unity in faith, witness and service for a just and peaceful world. A global fellowship, the WCC brings together 345 Protestant, Orthodox, Anglican and other churches representing more than 550 million Christians in 110 countries and works cooperatively with the Roman Catholic Church.

Opinions expressed in WCC Publications are those of the authors.

Scripture quotations are from the New Revised Standard Version Bible, © copyright 1989 by the Division of Christian Education of the National Council of the Churches of Christ in the USA. Used by permission.

Cover design: Julie Kauffman Design
Book design and typesetting: Michelle Cook / 4 Seasons Book Design
ISBN: 978-2-8254-1686-0

World Council of Churches
150 route de Ferney, P.O. Box 2100
1211 Geneva 2, Switzerland
http://publications.oikoumene.org

I BELONG

CONTENTS

PREFACE

SEMEGNISH ASFAW

More than ten million people in our world live without any nationality, without any legal existence. They are stateless, "legally invisible" individuals who, on a daily basis, face discrimination and marginalization in their lives. Most of the rights and entitlements that those of us who have a nationality take for granted are inaccessible to them: since they do not have any legal existence in the eyes of the law of any country in this world, in most cases they cannot own property, access education or healthcare, travel freely, etc. Basic social and political rights are often out of reach for stateless people: statelessness can easily become a recipe for vulnerability, a springboard for exploitation, injustice, and abuse.

Statelessness is mainly the result of discrimination: discrimination against members of a community because of their ethnic or religious affiliation. It can also be discrimination against women: currently, 27 countries in the world practise gender injustice in nationality laws, meaning that they do not allow women to pass nationality to their children on an equal basis with men. In combination with situations of international forced migration, this discrimination has the potential to create a generation of stateless children – if children are born without the presence of the father.

The World Council of Churches' (WCC) Pilgrimage of Justice and Peace, launched in 2013 during the WCC 10th Assembly in Busan, invited churches, ecumenical partners, and all members of the ecumenical family to embark on a journey of collaboration, mutual accountability, and solidarity in view of building just and inclusive communities in which justice and peace will prevail, according to the teachings of scripture. Stateless people –that is, sisters and brothers who have been marginalized and rendered vulnerable because they lack any legal link to a state – are among those communities on whose struggles the pilgrimage aims to shed light, bringing them back to the centre.

But what does the Bible teach us about caring for the vulnerable, the marginalized, and the forgotten members of our communities?

Speak out for those who cannot speak,
for the rights of all the destitute.
Speak out, judge righteously,
defend the rights of the poor and needy. (Prov. 31:8-9)

After all, the scriptures teach us that "those who oppress the poor insult their Maker, but those who are kind to the needy honor him" (Prov. 14:31).

This publication is a selection of biblical reflections on statelessness. They are introduced by three more general pieces: a theological overview based in biblical reflection, by Bishop De Chickera, a personal narrative of the experience of stateless from Hans Ucko, and an overview of the biblical reflections by Ani Ghazaryan Drissi. What follows then, in roughly canonical order, are nine further Bible stuides. Some are thematic, while many are contextual. We hope that they will be useful tools for discussion and reflection during Bible studies in congregations and communities around the world.

Semegnish Asfaw is programme executive in the area of public witness for the World Council of Churches, author of *The Invisible among Us: Hidden, Forgotten, Stateless,* and co-editor of *Responsibility to Protect and of Just Peace: Orthodox Perspectives.*

Daniel Ayuch is Professor of New Testament at the St. John of Damascus Institute of Theology at the University of Balamand, Tripoli, Lebanon, where he teaches courses in the field of New Testament studies. He is author of numerous articles in New Testament and biblical criticism.

Emmanuel Clapsis is the Archbishop Iakovos Professor of Orthodox Theology at Holy Cross School of Theology, Brookline, Massachusets, USA. Among his many works, he is author of *Orthodoxy in Conversation: Orthodox Ecumenical Engagements*

Duleep de Chickera is the now-retired Anglican Bishop of Colombo, Sri Lanka. A renowned preacher and a strong advocate for interreligious understanding and peacemaking, he is also co-editor of *The Anglican Way: Signposts for a Common Journey* (2014).

Shirley DeWolf *is* an ordained pastor in the United Methodist Church, Zimbabwe, a former university lecturer there, and a professional working in community organizing and with uprooted people.

Ani Ghazaryan Drissi is a programme executive in the WCC's Faith and Order Commission. Her doctoral work was in the area of patristic exegesis and New Testament. She also coordinates doctoral studies in theology at the University of Geneva.

Fernando Enns is Professor of Protestant Theology at the University of Hamburg and of the Theology and Ethics of Peace at the Free University of Amsterdam. A theologian in the tradition of the historic peace churches, he has also been a leader in the ecumenical movement for two decades. Among his many works is *Ökumene und Frieden* (2012). He is co-chair of the reference group for the WCC's Pilgrimage of Justice and Peace.

Guillermo Kerber, a Catholic theologian from Uruguay, served as WCC programme executive for Care for Creation and Climate Justice and supervised its work in Ecojustice and *Diakonia*. He has served on the boards of the Life and Peace Institute and Global Call for Climate Action, and he teaches in the Atelier Oecuménique de Théologie, Geneva.

Frankelly Martínez works for the international development NGO Christian Aid as a senior programme officer for the Dominican Republic.

Suzanne Membe-Matale, ordained in the African Methodist Episcopal Church, is general secretary of the Council of Churches in Zambia.

Evelyn L. Parker is Susanna Wesley Centennial Professor of Practical Theology and Associate Dean for Academic Affairs at Perkins School of Theology, Southern Methodist University, Fort Worth, Texas, USA. Among her publications is *Trouble Don't Last Always* (2003).

Elenie Poulos is a Minister of the Uniting Church in Australia. She was appointed National Director of UnitingJustice Australia and a past chair of the Australian Churches Refugee Taskforce.

Hans Ucko, ordained in the Church of Sweden, was longtime programme executive for the WCC's office on Interreligious Relations and Dialogue. Especially known for his work in Jewish-Christian relations, he is author of numerous books, including *Faces of the Other* (2005).

CHAPTER 1

TOWARD A THEOLOGY OF STATELESSNESS

DULEEP DE CHICKERA

The biblical concept of the alien

The Den Dolder Consultation (Netherlands, 2014) called for theological reflection and awareness on statelessness.[1] One useful entry point into such a theology, still in its infancy, is through the biblical concept of the alien,[2] and a useful way of approaching this concept of the biblical alien is through the Abrahamic narrative (see Gen. 11:27-36). This legendary narrative may be observed at two levels: the visible-obvious and the hidden-substantial. The visible-obvious is that of Abraham the nomadic wanderer moving from place to place with his extended family and their flocks in search of pasture. For them there was no fixed territory or demarcated boundaries[3]; their security was located in the freedom of movement. The hidden-substantial level indicates that this movement was at the direction of Yahweh, the God who had revealed God's self to Abraham and called him to be the founding father of a nation in a land set aside for him and his ancestors (Gen. 12 1-3). In the yet unseen and yet unknown lay the promise of nationhood for these

---

1. Such a quest begins with questions such as where is God in this human tragedy, what is God saying and what direction and life-giving options is God provoking and so on.

2. Not an intruder from Mars but the human outsider among us.

3. The instances of temporary migration that occurred were either because of prosperity (Gen. 13.8-13), or in crises such as famine (Gen. 12:10, Gen. 42:1-3).

nomadic wanderers on the sole condition of faithfulness to this one God, Yahweh.

More settled socio-cultural groups at that time perceived nomadic wanderers as those from beyond. They were considered strangers because they were different and had no territorial identity. They were viewed with suspicion (Gen. 46:34b) and had no access to whatever rights and privileges the settled community enjoyed. Located at the social fringes of life, they were easily termed aliens.

But this was not all. If the alien was asked where home was, they would answer everywhere. But when others settled and claimed land for their own and defined their boundaries, the wandering ones of everywhere, now overtaken, had nowhere to call their own. This consequently pushed them to the physical fringes of life[4] to become twice disadvantaged people like today's stateless of the world.

The early biblical image of the alien is therefore of a wandering people moving under the direction of God toward nationhood and a prescribed land. But at the same time, they were pushed to the social and physical fringes of life in a climate of land acquisition and territorial definition by other people, who had also moved toward nationhood based on defined boundaries.

Law and the prophets: Protection for the alien

The exodus provides the background to the Hebrew law on the alien. The status of the Hebrews settled in Egypt deteriorates drastically until they suffer the ultimate humiliation of slavery (Ex. 1:13-14; 2:23). The groans of these oppressed slaves are heard by Yahweh, who calls and commissions Moses to lead them out of bondage and away from Egypt. The movement from Egypt amounts to a reversal of status. The oppressed slaves are drawn into a covenant with God-Yahweh through Moses and resume their stalled journey toward the dignity and fulfilment of nation-identity (Ex. 12:37, 50; 13:17).

---

4. So, as we read in Joshua and Judges, the Israelites had to fight for the land as others had settled ahead of them.

It is during this journey from movement-identity toward nation-identity that Yahweh discloses the holiness code to the Hebrews (Lev. 19). The essence of this code is that Hebrew conduct and lifestyle are to reflect the character of the holy God who has delivered them from bondage (Lev. 19:2). It is within this wider teaching on several aspects of holiness that instruction is given on the treatment of aliens among the Hebrews. The content of teaching resembles a charter. It offers insights on the status and rights of the stateless and is a high point in Hebrew spirituality.

A substantial change is noticed in the charter-text on how aliens are referred to. They are no longer called strangers but resident aliens. Further, there is a double emphasis on inclusion, as the Hebrews are to treat the resident aliens as equals among them. "Native among you," "native born," "citizen among you," and "own countryman"[5] are some of the terms used by various translations of the Bible that strive to convey the idea of full inclusion.

As if this is not enough, the charter text makes a categorical requirement that the resident aliens are to be loved as the Hebrews love themselves. This amounts to unconditional acceptance and the surest guarantee against oppression, since love gives of oneself while oppression takes for oneself. The clarity of the charter-text leaves no room for exclusion or abuse of the resident aliens; neither is there room for misunderstanding or neglect.

The charter-text also includes a rationale for the complete inclusion of the resident aliens. The Hebrews are to remember that they were slaves in Egypt and refrain from treating others similarly. The memory of alienation in Egypt is to provoke a contrasting behaviour of inclusion. Elsewhere this rationale is set out in empathetic language. The Hebrews are to include the resident aliens because "you know the heart of an alien" (Ex. 23:9). Even if individuals among the Hebrews behaved to the contrary or called for a different reaction, the collective historical pain was to prevail for proper conduct and inclusion.

---

5. See RSV, ESV, NIV, Green Bible, Jerusalem Bible.

Finally, the charter-text attaches a stamp of authority to the inclusive treatment of the resident aliens. "I am the Lord your God," is none other than the God experienced in distress (Ps. 18:6; 50:152). God is not an unknown God, but a God of generosity and saving power. The Hebrews are therefore to continue to trust God's requirement, as it can only be in line with the wider unfolding covenant promise.

A summary of this charter-text on the treatment of the resident aliens highlights four key features; the principle of total equality, the practice of total inclusion, the rationale of contrast hardship, and the authority of a God who delivered the Hebrews from bondage.

The collective Hebrew convention on the treatment of the resident aliens in their midst is set out briefly under different types of security. These are the following:

1. Food security (Lev. 19:9, 10; 23:22; Deut. 24:19, 20). Not all produce is to be gathered at harvest time. Some of it is to be left for the resident aliens.

2. Constitutional security (Lev 24:22; Ex. 12:49). There is to be one law for both the citizen and resident aliens.

3. Justice security (Deut. 1:16, 17). Both citizens and resident aliens are to be given a fair hearing by judges.

4. Religious security (Num. 15:15, 16; Deut. 20:10-12). The citizen and the resident aliens are equal before the law, within the covenant and before God.

5. Moral security (Deut. 27:19; Mal. 3:5). The resident aliens is not to be thrust away from justice and those who deprive them of justice are cursed.

6. Social security (Ps. 94:3-7). There is protest when the resident aliens are subject to violence.

7. Spiritual security (Jer. 7:5-7). The absence of oppression in the treatment of the resident aliens facilitates the presence of God.

Interim comments

The cluster indicates an ascending grid ranging from physical protection offered the resident aliens to the gift of grace that the presence of the resident aliens brings. Since the inclusive treatment of the resident aliens ensures the collective integrity of Israel, there is value in the real presence of the resident aliens, now no more a liability. When the inclusion of the resident aliens is in place, there is a flourishing of democracy that spills over among the surrounding nations. This takes the form of cities of refuge and protection for fugitives from other nations (Josh. 20:2f; Is. 16:3-5). The mandate here is radically humane and has eschatological connotations, as outlaws from elsewhere are to be settled in Israel until oppressors and marauders are no more and a throne of righteousness is in place. There is a subversive side to this political hospitality too, as fugitives are to be hidden in order that they may be saved. Hebrew law and convention on the alien is therefore both progressive and life giving.[6] They offer a model of community integration for citizens by birth as well as those naturalized.

Return to oppression

This is, however, not the end of the story. The post-monarchical period paints a different picture. A census (2 Chron. 2:17f) during Solomon's reign numbers the aliens in Israel at 153,600[7] and describes their work as hard labour and cutters of stone under the supervision of their very own overseers. Rather than remembering Egypt to avoid oppressing the alien, the Israelites had chosen to remember and do exactly likewise.

The reason for this complete reversal is best explained through the territorial expansionism and unprecedented extravagant lifestyle of sections of the Israelites under Solomon (2 Chron. 8:1-10). Such advancements always come at a price, and this is usually the exploitation of the underclass. As the

---

6. This inclusion of the alien is, however, based on two conditions: the rejection of idolatry and circumcision. The place of such religio-cultural neutralization in exchange for security and stability is an area for further investigation and study.

7. Said to be a tenth of the total population of Israel.

text describes, the exploitation of aliens in their midst[8] was necessary for the economic excesses and achievements under Solomon.

The prophets

Nevertheless God's just ways manifest through a resilient Hebrew spirituality, yet provide a deterrent to the violation of the charter-text on the resident aliens. This comes with the emergence of the prophets and the prophetic tradition, which primarily and relentlessly called for economic justice and an end to exploitation.[9] This implies that charters, laws, and constitutions, however noble, cannot stand by themselves. They need voices that remind, interpret, and insist on the equal and just belonging of all.[10] Such voices, however, are to stand in line with the prophetic tradition and speak truth with courage.

Jesus and the disadvantaged outsider

During the time of Jesus, there is no reference to aliens[11] as outsiders, but categories such as Samaritans and tax collectors were considered social outcasts (Luke 5:30; John. 4:7-9). Occasionally the outsider was referred to as the foreigner (Luke 17:18). The Jews considered these outcasts unworthy of covenantal membership.

Two memorable secular events that surrounded the birth of Jesus require some comment: the Roman census that took Mary and Joseph to Bethlehem and Herod's death sentence on male babies that resulted in the family seeking refuge in Egypt. These events – the calculative as well as the

---

8. From which the citizens were exempt.

9. The recurring call of the prophets of the 8th BCE was for an end to accumulation and oppression – both manifestations of economic injustice.

10. It was voices that made the recent changes in Sri Lanka possible. This was in spite of a fairly inclusive constitution being in place. The antidote to modern manipulative politics is none other than the voice of the people.

11. The term, however, takes on a purely theological connotation that refers to humans in sin as aliens from the household of God. See Eph. 2:7-20.

brutal – are different manifestations of styles of oppressive governance by civil authorities.

Nevertheless there are profound theological insights of an incarnational, redemptive, and eschatological nature that rise through these negative thrusts. Given the Roman practice of household registration at a census, the birth of Jesus is officially registered. This way, God's unique act of entering human history as a human is recorded among humans in human history. With this, birth registration, the right of every child and parent, becomes a human right enjoyed by the human Jesus in whom God was present in fullness.

Also, the ruthless murder of male babies at the birth of Jesus takes away any illusions of a protected incarnation. God does not merely enter human history through Jesus but plunges into the brutal realities of human power struggles, indicating that the new life being initiated through a new creation was compelled to rise out of the chaotic events of history. Hence the stage was set at the birth of Jesus for the encounter between sacrificial love that prompted the incarnation and the resistance and evil machinations of the greed for power at all cost. Consequently, windows open to the inevitability of the cross in the quest for a better world and with it a hope that the work of recovery begun at the incarnation will reach completion sometime in the future.

It is in this tension of God at work in the midst of human affairs (the incarnation) and the oppressive obstacles imposed by humans to this initiative of sacrificial love (the cross) that we are to craft a way forward to that day when just integration will be restored (eschatological hope) and all disadvantaged outsiders will be treated with equal dignity and justice.

This background facilitates a review of Jesus' attitude to the disadvantaged outsiders. Two face-to-face encounters and two parables adequately demonstrate this attitude.[12]

---

12. So do the several other encounters between Jesus and other disadvantaged outsiderss recorded in the gospels.

The encounter with the Samaritan leper: Luke 17:11-18

When this twice disadvantaged human returns to thank God for healing grace, Jesus draws attention to his covenantal behaviour by commending the Samaritan's demonstration of gratitude. The question "Where are the nine?" (Luke 17:17-18) contrasts this covenantal behaviour of the excluded with the absence of covenantal behaviour in those who claim allegiance within the covenant.

In this dual public stance of commendation and critique, Jesus reverses the false and hurtful assumptions of the day to reconstruct and announce that God includes the excluded and calls for a review of the hypocrisy of those who confer inclusion on themselves to the exclusion of others. If through behaviour the outcast is within the circle of grace, then the hypocrisy of hierarchical social exclusion comes under judgment.

The encounter with the woman at the well: John 4:19-24

As her self-confidence is restored by Jesus – a male Jew asking water of a Samaritan woman – the woman is able to rise to an equal conversation on the delicate question of traditions of worship. It is as the exclusive temple tradition of the covenant people and exclusive mountain tradition of the extra-covenantal Samaritans engage each other that the inclusive truth of worship is revealed. Indeed God is worshiped (in spirit and in truth) beyond these exclusive locations wherever there is a desire for truth over tradition and the freedom of the spirit over space.

In this encounter, Jesus' revelation comes in two connected steps: first, it is in the meeting of the limited understandings of all truth that an elevation into more substantial truth is possible; and second, the more radical step, that the truth perspective of the outcast brings a value of its own that adds clarification to the reservoir of truth within the covenant. In this instance, the truth is regarding the primary and unchanging purpose of all creation: the worship of the Creator. To leave the stranger cast out of the truth equation is consequently detrimental to the covenant and closes the door in the common human quest.

In a nutshell these teaching encounters clearly convey that God is at work among all cultures and human endeavour, and that this reality extinguishes the superficial human distinction between inclusive and exclusive communities.

The parable of the good samaritan: Luke 10:25-37

Continuing on these lines, Jesus shifts to his most radical teaching on the disadvantaged outsiders. The conversation and questions that precede and lead to the narration of this parable focus on the core kingdom spirituality of love for neighbour. Adherence to this command is an indispensable ingredient of the covenant. Its violation amounts to sin.

As the parable unravels it becomes clear that not only do the disadvantaged outsider strangers demonstrate this essential covenantal spirituality, but that those within the covenant are to follow the example of those they have excluded if they are to recover their lost spirituality and remain in the covenant. Put differently, the parable asserts that God has kept alive the central spirituality of the covenant people among those excluded from the covenant because the covenantal people had come to compromise the essence of this spirituality by refusing to love and include the disadvantaged outsiders. The covenantal obedience of the excluded stranger is thus a life-giving, even sacramental, presence in circumstances of religious arrogance and sustains hope for the common good, unlike the chosen ones who spread contempt to dislocate human community. If the stateless were to be included in the beatitudes Jesus would announce; "Blessed are those at the margins for they point the way to truth and life."

The parable of the last judgment: Matthew 25:31-45

This parable has been understood in a limited way across the generations to suggest that good works that relieve human suffering are the criteria for continuing communion in God. Its thrust goes far beyond this, however, to articulate a dramatic example of secular spirituality. The ones who respond to human need are surprised to learn that Jesus is present in an inseparable way with and among the world's vulnerable, and it is consequently in this inseparable integration of the vulnerable and Jesus that communion in God is sustained and ensured.

Here then is another radical edge to the gospel; those who dwell among the vulnerable dwell in Jesus and those in Jesus cannot but be amidst the vulnerable. It is in the very excluded and shunned fringes of life – considered untouchable and contaminated and too lost, forlorn, and inappropriate for human dwelling – that God in Jesus dwells. This calls for a rearrangement of human values and relationships that eliminates distinctions of inclusion and exclusion and affirms the sharing and celebration of a common life in God and the other.

Implications for statelessness

Even though exclusion, rejection, and humiliation characterize the wanderings of the stateless, God's option for the vulnerable disadvantaged suggests that God is present at a more substantial level with the stateless. They have not been abandoned; rather God accompanies and journeys with the stateless toward the dignity and stability of national identity.

What matters in this journey of encounter is the humanity of the vulnerable. It is this humanity above all else that justifies the dignity of nation-identity and is a corollary to being made as humans in the image of God.

God is the source of the law: a collective code for proper conduct that ensures just integration for all, both citizen and guest, within a socio-cultural entity. But the law cannot stand alone. It is to be held under constant scrutiny and review; if not, it can be compromised, manipulated, abused, and distorted to the advantage of some, usually the powerful and the greedy.

So God raises prophets: to draw attention to the compromise and call for a return to the objective of the law – just integration for all.

Since bad laws and distorted justice can become a way of life, the presence and voice of prophets too, as the conscience of a people, are to become a counter way of life. Consequently, an alert civil society is essential for just integration since the best laws in the world are of little use if there is no accompanying social surveillance.

Review and critique should be continuing features of the democratic society. These impulses for just systems and order come from within the human made in God's image. They are nourished and passed on through institutions and practices that uphold the values and vision of just integration for all. The protection of these institutions and practices is therefore a sacred task conferred on every generation.

When good laws are compromised or bad laws passed, people of conscience are to take sides, resist, and work for the restoration of just integration with truth and courage. The objective of social justice, however, is inclusive reconciliation: where there is healing space for both the grieved victim as well as the repentant oppressor.

The law is not infinite. As and when human need and contingencies change and new challenges emerge, the law is required to adapt through reform to meet the aspirations of humans caught up these complex realities. The law (international as well as domestic) has no other purpose apart from serving the common good. Prophets and advocates who stand with the stateless are to never grow tired of legal reform that will reverse the status and conditions of the vulnerable disadvantaged in our midst.

God works even through the devices and strategies of oppressive regimes to bring to completion God's designs for stateless disadvantaged outsiderss. This includes birth registration: a right that can emerge from forces working for the wrong objectives. The Caesars and Herods of our world are passing stages of interference. They are never to be allowed to have the last word.

Jesus brings stateless disadvantaged outsiders to the centre of the discourse to highlight their plight as well as their value and dignity. He does this through incarnational association and prophetic teaching so that all may rise to a life of inclusion.

Long before postmodernism claimed that truth was at the periphery also, Jesus taught that truth is where there is human community, and in particular vulnerable human community. He much more emphasized that stateless disadvantaged outsiders have a resilience and spirituality that enrich others, especially their oppressors. When this is recognized all stand to be transformed and the common good benefits. Sustained exclusion is consequently detrimental to those who exclude others.

Finally, Jesus' clear answer is a resounding yes to the protection, prevention, and reduction of statelessness. He however goes further. If we dare to immerse ourselves in the lives of the stateless disadvantaged outsiders, this will trigger a common rising and the elimination of statelessness.

CHAPTER 2

STATELESSNESS: A PERSONAL REFLECTION

HANS UCKO

My father never referred to anything religious. "Oh, please," he would say when someone brought God into the conversation, "please, leave God out of this." It was almost as if he felt sorry for God and understood the danger if God were to be brought into any reflection or conversation on matters of real concern. "*Lasst doch den lieben Gott allein!*" he would say. Leave the poor God out of this; he won't be able to handle it! If we can't deal with it, how can we expect God to cope or manage our wretched reality? And if the talk was on the Holocaust, he was precise about it. Leave God out of it! What did God do for anyone of us who survived the Holocaust? He was silent about those who died in the Holocaust. He never mentioned the dead. Not even his mother. I asked questions all the time about the last months or days of the victims. How was their last hour and where was God? He never asked that question.

And he never answered my questions. I looked in his photo album and saw people and knew without asking that there were many who had succumbed, who were no more, relatives, friends and acquaintances. I knew some by name. I looked at the photo of his mother. She was my grandmother, although to me it was as if she had never lived. She was only someone who was transported away, in some kind of unending transport. My father was alone. He had been left to survive. Going from country to country looking for a country that would accept the refugee that he now was; maybe he was thinking of his mother as you would think about a mother, with love and longing.

Alien in a new land

The country that finally received him remained as alien to him as he was to it. It was never to be his. It was strange from the beginning; and even 40 years later, when he had become a national of this country, they hadn't really met. It wasn't just settling in a new country, whether they opened wide the gates or just left the gates ajar. As much as I could see it, the present and the future clouded his days. Since he never talked about the past, I often wondered who gave him the impulse to leave his country, to flee and leave it all behind, to save his life. How did he know when to leave and where to go? He wasn't much of an analyst, one who would sit down and calculate pros and cons. And he was above all German. Wilhelm was his name, like the Kaiser.

Maybe my father had a dream in early 1938 and in that dream an angel appeared to him and told him to leave Germany. It had happened before: "Now after they had left, an angel of the Lord appeared to Joseph in a dream and said, "Get up, take the child and his mother, and flee to Egypt, and remain there until I tell you; for Herod is about to search for the child, to destroy him." (Matt. 2:13).

Icons and paintings portray Mary and Joseph in the middle of their flight as remarkably composed. There is no fear in their eyes. Maybe because of the angel. I will always remember my father having fear in his eyes. There was a Herod in his life, although his name was Hitler. I wonder whether there ever was an angel in his dreams. I think his mother told him: "Dear Helmi, you must leave Germany; your *Vaterland* is about to destroy you. It will be dangerous for you to stay. I'm too old but you at least must flee that you may live." A couple of years later she was transported away into the night of destruction at Treblinka. And from those days, fear was always in his eyes.

Because of Herod, Mary and Joseph became refugees and reached Egypt. They look so calm. Was there a Jewish community receiving them, making their life in Egypt almost like their previous life in the country they had had to leave? The flight to Egypt was a popular subject in art. Paintings show the holy family protected by all during their time as refugees. In the Apocrypha, palm trees bow before the infant Jesus, the beasts of the desert pay him homage. A spring gushes up from the desert and a date palm tree bends down to allow them to pluck its fruit. Trees and fields shield them from enemies. Their time as refugees was not long and the angel told them when they could return. Neither the biblical text nor the Apocrypha has anything to say about the plight of really being a refugee. We will not read about the panic, the fear of being caught; there will be no mention of the worry, of asking over and over again where it will be possible to end the running away and to find a place to stay.

My father "was a wandering Aramean" (Deut. 26:5); he was a refugee from Germany and there was no angel to whisper in his ear when to leave or when to return. Hell broke loose in Germany and he went to Sweden and lived there as an alien and he couldn't cry to the Lord, the God of his ancestors, because he had understood that the Lord didn't hear his voice or see his affliction, toil, and oppression and that his mother was not allowed to enter Sweden but was taken away to the concentration camp.

My father never found his way in Sweden. He carried with him the passport of the stateless – the Nansen passport – an international substitute for a passport that allowed stateless persons or those deprived of their national passports to enter other countries. But he was not allowed to define himself. His identity as German was strictly downgraded and the identity as stateless took over the whole. Others defined him and said who he was: a stateless refugee by the name of Wilhelm Israel. He tried to protest saying that Israel was not at all his name. It was the name Hitler had given all German male Jews. But the Nansen passport didn't see a German man holding the passport at all. Next to the photo in the Nansen passport it simply stated that which was now his sole identity: a Jewish refugee by the name of Wilhelm Israel. And he was stateless.

He now had a residence permit and he didn't have to flee anymore. But a stateless person doesn't legally exist; the state system doesn't see him. He's invisible, marginalized, forgotten, as if hidden, although living visibly among those who were the people of the land, nationals, those who belonged. He was now to begin the long process of trying to become visible again, but as someone who could no longer refer to his origins as who he really was. It was a long journey, which begins with eyes full of fears and which has many obstacles, as he was about to shed the vulnerability and defencelessness of being stateless.

"By the rivers of Babylon – there we sat down and there we wept when we remembered Zion" (Ps. 137). At the shores of the strait of Öresund, my father was weeping, because he was homesick for Germany. He was free, he had found refuge, he had even found a job, although not as the photographer he was, because Sweden feared that he might use the camera for espionage; he was given a job as a menial worker. He was not alone; he now had a wife and a child. He had begun to learn the new language. It went very slow because he was weeping, as he was often remembering Germany. This was the country that had murdered his mother and many relatives and friends. This was the country that had made him a second-class citizen, that had made him flee the country, running from country to country. And yet this was the country he was longing for: its people, its language, its history, its culture.

Now he was living in freedom, he had a job, he had a family – and yet, he was weeping. Every Sunday morning he put me on his lap and we tried to find the German broadcast station on the radio and he would explain Mozart and Beethoven as he hummed along. There were those among our relatives and friends who had also survived the Holocaust, who had pledged never to go to Germany, and to even avoid travelling through Germany. But my father would take me as a young boy and travel by train around in Germany, from place to place, and we would take photos outside castles and in front of monuments. He would order food specific to different regions: from Kartoffelklöße to Königsberger Klopse and from Mohnkuchen to Streußelkuchen. He would sing along with all the Germans on the boat, as we were traveling down the river and passed the Lorelei, the high, steep slate rock on the right bank of the River Rhine:

Ich weiß nicht was soll es bedeuten,
Dass ich so traurig bin;
Ein Märchen aus uralten Zeiten,
Das kommt mir nicht aus dem Sinn

I know not if there is a reason
Why I am so sad at heart.
A legend of bygone ages
Haunts me and will not depart.

Maybe the song communicated that deep sadness of never being able to forget his country, despite its Nazi past. This is the insidious burden of being rejected by your country and unable to stop loving it. He carried his country with him every day. There was a veil over his eyes. It was as if he was in a haze, and he couldn't see what was plainly there in the new country: possibility and a future. He was tied to his country, and the older he grew, the more he returned in his mind to those days in Germany when there was no Hitler or Gestapo but only his mother and siblings and their little photo atelier. You could take the Jew out of Germany, but you couldn't take Germany out of the Jew!

A doctor examined him and asked him about his sadness and the fear in his eyes and said, "You suffer from 'uprootedness'-depression." As a stateless person, who ultimately was granted citizenship in the new country, he had to embark upon a daily struggle to construct a new identity. It was not a given. Constructing a new identity, he had to put aside the identity that had been one with his country of origin – its culture, language, and history – but that also had perpetrated a crime against his family. And in the construction of a new identity, one experiences inferiority, racism, loneliness, marginalization, and the depression that is evoked by the feeling of being constantly "in-between." Some can embrace the hybridity or the mixing of different cultures. He couldn't. And because he couldn't divorce himself from his real identity, the new identity was never solid enough to withstand the feelings of uprootedness. Hence, you sit there by the rivers of Babylon, where you are imprisoned and long for Zion; or you are at the straits of Öresund, which has offered you a place to stay as a refuge from the ravages of Nazism and anti-Semitism; or you cruise along the Rhine by Lorelei, back in the old country, realizing how much a part of it you are despite the gruesome killings. And the memories come rushing in over you and you understand that statelessness will follow you long into your new identity and nationality, and it will never let go of the hold it has on you.

> *Vindicate me, O Lord, for I have walked in my integrity, and I have trusted in the Lord without wavering. Prove me, O Lord, and try me; test my heart and mind. For your steadfast love is before my eyes, and I walk in faithfulness to you. (Ps. 26)*

Restitution, reparation, reconciliation

There's an affinity with statelessness in my own personality. There is a sense of uncertainty that reverberates in me, a memory of that which cannot be remembered and yet remains as a sentiment. Not only because of a more or less conscious empathy and affinity with that part of my father's history, but because I was, remarkably or strangely enough, also registered as stateless at the time of my birth. According to the law, I should have been registered as a Swedish citizen, because a child acquires Swedish citizenship at birth if the child's mother is a Swedish citizen. But the young pastor recording the birth of the child put me together with my father in the registry books, and the two of us were stateless. It was only at the age of four that I, together with my father, acquired Swedish citizenship.

Some 50 years later, my father and I were again facing common citizenship, but now in relation to the only country of my father, Germany. Following the passing of my father, his home town emerged from the darkness of his forced departure. Together with my children, I obtained German citizenship and we were reconnected with the place that had seen him flee the Nazi regime as a stateless person. Germany's constitution, the Basic Law, stated that anyone who had had their German citizenship revoked during the Nazi regime for "political, racist, or religious reasons" could re-obtain citizenship, and it also applied to the descendants of Nazi victims. It was in the spirit of *Vergangenheitsbewältigung*, the process of coming to terms with the past, that Germany remembered my father and in an act of reparation gave me German citizenship.

Other more or less similar circumstances around the world call for such a spirit and such intentional action. Throughout the world we see similar needs for restitution. In my father's case, it was an act of reparation, albeit posthumously. It is in German called *Wiedergutmachung*, literally, an act of making well again. Historically, the original term signified that the German state, in an act of reparation, declared itself prepared to compensate victims of Nazism. Posthumously, my father was now, through us, restored as a German citizen and reconnected to the place he was born. The act had deep symbolic meaning and recognition. The stateless one was again recognized as a citizen. It is significant when a government tries to restore the dignity and hope of stateless people. It is never too late. It can change the lives of the stateless. It is about recognition, about restoring belongingness, recognizing the personhood of those who were once made invisible, who were non-persons.

Stateless people are ontologically harmed when they are deprived of their fundamental human qualities, such as their rights and responsibilities. A stateless person's limited agency or ability to act reduces their potential as a human being. The plight of stateless people – insecurity, fear, uncertainty, the risk of exploitation – is a concern for everyone: people of different religions as well as people of no religion. It's a global concern; more than ten million people around the world live without any nationality: they are state-less people. It's a question of ethics. Statelessness destroys on several levels. Loss of citizenship has legal and political consequences, not only for the one who is stateless but also for society and the human community. Every sector of society needs to ask itself whether it can avoid its obligation toward people who are living more or less permanently outside the nation-state system and for whose well-being no state acknowledges political or moral responsibility. Society must ask itself about the moral obligation to admit refugees, and also ask whether we can morally justify closing our borders. Society in its various manifestations must ask whether the discourse can be limited to the question of admission. Is it enough to discuss whether state-less people are eligible for admission to the new country? Hasn't society failed to consider the obligations it may have to people who remain outside of society and its communities for prolonged periods of time?

"He has told you, O mortal, what is good; and what does the Lord require of you but to do justice, and to love kindness, and to walk humbly with your God?" (Micah 6:8). Religion mustn't fail to create believers or followers who care for their fellow neighbour. My father's concern to leave God out of it was probably based on seeing religion fail. Religion must emerge from the reductive view that sees it either as the major source of conflict and war in the world or, as per the apologists, as whitewashed from the violence perpetrated in its name.

Religions are designed to confront ethical indifference among believers. A religious person is not supposed to stand idly by while another is in pain or distress – and yet something about religion itself seems to be a catalyst, under certain circumstances, for creating the very indifference it seeks to banish. Believing in a perfectly good and transcendent God can lead a person to ignore the needs of lesser, mortal, terrestrial beings. Religion mustn't shut down our moral instincts to such an extent that we no longer see things as they are but only see that which we think must be offensive to God.

There is in religion also the temptation to claim the all-powerful transcendent God for petty human disputes and institutions. This is when religious people cloak themselves in the grace of God, defining God as being with us regardless of what we do or deserve, attributing pious motivation and religious value to all of our behaviour. Once we can no longer see who we have become, we will have lost the ability to self-correct and to repent. There are those who have lost their moral compass completely.

Recognizing that members of a religious community are something like God's ambassadors on earth – and in order to make God's name great on earth – we have to be good ambassadors who live lives of moral rectitude that put the needs of others first. In other words, in order to put God first, we have to put God second. By putting people first, irrespective of their beliefs or practices, as ambassadors of God we make God's name great.

My father was not a religious person and his *"Lasst doch den lieben Gott allein"* was a way of saying that being human is sufficient and is hard enough in itself to live up to. Shoulder your responsibility as a human being and don't hide or take refuge in God-talk. The the letters *G*, *O*, and *D* need to be carefully detached from one another to enable us to see beyond them and to realize that letters put together in a given order easily become something you can hide behind. It is in the nature of things that expressions of ultimate concern vanish and may be replaced. Symbols, which formerly expressed the truth of faith for some, now remind us more of the faith of the past. They have lost their truth. The most important symbol that has lost its ultimate truth is perhaps the primordial symbol of God, which, after Hitler, was irrevocably undermined for those who had to live through those times and particularly for people who had lost their loved ones in the Holocaust.

These survivors had to walk a difficult path because there was no light along the way. Everything was dark night. There was no quick fix, no immediate comfort zone. They really had to walk "through the darkest valleys" (Ps. 23), and only there, if you were careful, might you become aware that you are not walking alone. You might, on your way, walk alongside and pass the huddled masses, every one of them yearning to breathe free. And you begin to see that they, in strange ways, each carry a letter of the name of the ultimate or divine.

So many letters, so many possibilities created through so many people putting them together in constantly shifting order and sequences!

For Further Reflection

1. There was one recurring phrase in the public discourse after the extermination of millions of Jews, Roma, homosexuals, and others. It has almost become a classic in its German version: *"Wir wussten nichts davon!"* we didn't know anything about it! How much Germans knew about what was happening is still debated. That is not the issue here. What is an issue is that, since the Holocaust, we know so much more about what is happening around us and in the world. Social media have made knowledge about what is happening available to an unprecedented degree. In almost all parts of the world we are also, through social media, invited to participate, to like or dislike, to associate and to dissociate ourselves from various events.

We can no longer say, "We had no idea!" In hindsight, it will not be enough to use emoticons. It may make us feel good, but does it do good?

Therefore, in the light of the fact that there are ten million stateless people in the world today, what does it mean that we no longer can say: "We didn't know anything about it"? What is our responsibility?

2. Maybe religion has always lived with the temptation to co-opt God, the Divine, the Absolute, into becoming a servant of one's own ambitions. Today this seems to have become more visible than before; we see it in all religions. God is said to sanction, even bless, evil things done in the name of religion.

The author writes: "In order to put God first, we have to put God second. By putting people first, irrespective of their beliefs or practices, as ambassadors of God we make God's name great." Similar reflections have been expressed in different ways, all addressing the relationship of God and human, the other and me. The Danish theologian N. F. S. Grundtvig wrote: *"Menneske først og Christen saa"* ("First a human being, then a Christian"). The Turkish imam Fethullah Gülen wrote that there is an obligation for Muslims "to critically review our understanding and practice of Islam, in the light of the conditions and requirements of our age and the clarifications provided by our collective historic experiences." The poet and philosopher Samuel Coleridge wrote: "He, who begins by loving Christianity better than truth, will proceed by loving his own sect or church better than Christ, and end by loving himself better than all." What would these thoughts imply in my relation to stateless people, and what would it mean for the self-understanding of my own religiosity?

CHAPTER 3

THE CHURCH IS LIKE THE HOMELAND: A BIBLICAL REFLECTION

ANI GHAZARYAN DRISSI

Then the king will say to those at his right hand, "Come, you that are blessed by my Father, inherit the kingdom prepared for you from the foundation of the world; for I was hungry and you gave me food, I was thirsty and you gave me something to drink, I was a stranger and you welcomed me. (Matt. 25:34-35)

Be hospitable to one another without complaining. Like good stewards of the manifold grace of God, serve one another with whatever gift each of you has received. (1 Pet. 4:9-10).

When an alien resides with you in your land, you shall not oppress the alien. The alien who resides with you shall be to you as the citizen among you; you shall love the alien as yourself, for you were aliens in the land of Egypt: I am the Lord your God. (Lev. 19:33-34)

O Lord, who may abide in your tent? Who may dwell on your holy hill? Those who walk blamelessly, and do what is right, and speak the truth from their heart; who do not slander with their tongue, and do no evil to their friends, nor take up a reproach against their neghbours; in whose eyes the wicked are

despised, but who honour those who fear the Lord; who stand by their oath
even to their hurt; who do not lend money at interest, and do not take a bribe
against the innocent. (Ps. 15)

To be stateless is to be without nationality or citizenship. According to Article 1 of the 1954 United Nations High Commissioner for Refugees (UNHCR) Convention relating to the Status of Stateless Persons, a stateless person is one whom no state considers as a national by operation of its law. In this case, the legal bond between a state and an individual ceases to exist. Stateless people face many difficulties in their daily lives. People who are not recognized as citizens by any country usually have neither identity papers nor travel documents. Most of them have no access to basic rights, since these are often linked to nationality. A stateless child cannot in principle go to school, study or work legally, or travel. In some countries, people who have no identity papers are routinely imprisoned.

Entire populations can live on the margins of society, without papers or recognition, in injustice, but with the hope of being identified in the near future. What is the Bible's answer to the questions in relation to the status of these people? How do the Old and New Testaments introduce these poor and distressed people, and what place are they given in the scriptures? A brief journey through the Bible will enable us to know that even if the term "statelessness" is modern, the reality of people living without law and nationality is not. Such people have a long history, and the scriptures speak about them!

The biblical legacy

For the definition of this status, we find in the Bible words like "foreign," "passing stranger," "enemy," "alien": a native, but one whose existence is less associated with the locals. In the Old Testament the people of Israel were themselves foreigners in Egypt: "You shall not wrong or oppress a resident alien, for you were aliens in the land of Egypt" (Ex. 22:21). Thus, the people of Israel, previously stateless, received from the Lord a territory occupied by other people.

With this important heritage it is necessary to note that the people of Israel received the same divine order not to forget their status before and especially not to exploit and oppress the emigrant: "You shall not oppress a resident alien; you know the heart of an alien, for you were aliens in the land of Egypt" (Ex. 23:9). Thus, remembering that they were once foreigners in Egypt, the people of Israel must not be content simply to offer "residents" hospitality, but must love them as themselves: "When an alien resides with you in your land, you shall not oppress the alien. The alien who resides with you shall be to you as the citizen among you; you shall love the alien as yourself, for you were aliens in the land of Egypt: I am the Lord your God" (Lev. 19:33-34). God blesses outsiders, extending his protection to the needy and the poor: a God "who executes justice for the orphan and the widow, and who loves the strangers, providing them with food and clothing" (Deut. 10:18). He fixed them a legal status similar to the people of Israel (Deut. 1:16; Lev. 20:2), authorizing especially the circumcised to participate in the Passover (Ex. 12:48f), to observe the Sabbath (Ex. 20:10), to fast on the Day of Atonement (Lev. 16:29), and to not blaspheme the name of Yahweh (Lev. 24:16). Their assimilation is such that in the Israel of the end time, Ezekiel gives them the country to share with citizens by birth: "You shall allot it as an inheritance for yourselves and for the aliens who reside among you and have begotten children among you. They shall be to you as citizens of Israel; with you they shall be allotted an inheritance among the tribes of Israel. In whatever tribe aliens reside, there you shall assign them their inheritance, says the Lord God" (Ezek. 47:22-23).

God thus remains the true owner of the promised land (Gen. 12:1.7), and Israelites are aliens residing there: "The land shall not be sold in perpetuity, for the land is mine; with me you are but aliens and tenants" (Lev. 25:23). This idea contains a spiritual attitude that is found in the Psalms. The Israelite knows he has no rights in front of God, he only wants to be God's host (Ps. 15); the Israelite recognizes a foreign home, that he is a passer-by, like all his ancestors (Ps. 39:13; 1 Chron. 29:15). Also, passing in the other direction, he knows that his life on earth is brief; so he asks God to help him promptly: "I live as an alien in the land; do not hide your commandments from me" (Ps. 119:19).

An adaptation of the condition of residing abroad survives even in the Christian faith. In the New Testament, the intelligence of the human condition deepens further. The Christian has no permanent dwelling (2 Cor. 5:1f); they are strangers on earth not only because it belongs to God alone, but because they themselves are citizens of the heavenly homeland: there is neither host nor stranger, but all are fellow citizens of the saints: "So then you are no longer strangers and aliens, but you are citizens with the saints and also members of the household of God" (Eph. 2:19). Until Christians reach this term, their lives are journeying lives (1 Pet. 2:11), in imitation of that of the patriarchs (Heb. 11:13), who once tore themselves away from their land to journey to a better country (Heb. 11:16). The evangelist John accentuates the contrast between the world in which we must live and real life to which we are already introduced. Born from above (John 3:7), the Christian cannot be a stranger or pilgrim on this earth, because agreement is impossible between the Christian and the world: the world, in fact, is in the power of the evil one (1 John 5:19). But if it is not from this world, the Christian knows, as Christ, where he comes from and where he goes: he follows Christ who pitched his tent among us (John 1:14) and returned to the Father (16:28), who prepares a place for his family (14:2f): "Whoever serves me must follow me, and where I am, there will my servant be also. Whoever serves me, the Father will honor" (John 12:26).

As we can see, in the Bible, the message is clear: Do not just accept that the human being in this world has a host status and do not be content to exercise hospitality toward "residents," but love them as yourself. We read in the evangelist Matthew (25:34-35): "For I was hungry and you gave me food, I was thirsty and you gave me something to drink, I was a stranger and you welcomed me, I was naked and you gave me clothing, I was sick and you took care of me, I was in prison and you visited me." This love and hospitality are next to charity. In fact, through the host, it is Christ who is welcomed or repelled, recognized or disregarded, as indeed was the case with Jesus himself: not only at birth, when there was no place for him at the inn (Luke 2:7), but to the very end of his life, the world misunderstood him and his own people did not receive him (John 1:9ff).

Today: the Armenian example

Today millions of people are strangers in the eyes of the those amongst whom they live. We hear stories of human beings subjected to genocide, massacres, displacement, and floods. Here, as an Armenian, I must mention the memory of 1.5 million children and women, men and older people, massacred and deported in 1915. As a result of this genocide, millions of Armenians found refuge in the world. For some the welcome was somewhat successful; for others, the path was harder. Many Armenians, especially the first generation after the genocide, also remained stateless for life.

In the early 1920s, more than two million Armenians and Russians became stateless. First, the young Turkish republic banned the survivors of the 1915 genocide from returning; then they were deprived of their citizenship by Vladimir Lenin. Outraged by their situation, Norwegian Fridtjof Nansen (1861–1930), a scientist appointed High Commissioner for Refugees by the League of Nations, imposed an international administrative document – called "Nansen Passport" – which gave them identity and rights. After Armenians and Russians, other communities benefited from this famous certificate up to the beginning of World War II: the Jews deported by Nazi Germany, but also Spanish Republicans fleeing the Franco dictatorship. The Nansen Passport was issued during the interwar period to 450,000 people, including members of the former minorities of the Ottoman Empire. This document allowed the beneficiaries to avoid being stateless, to travel freely, to have rights, and ultimately to integrate into their host countries. Fridtjof Nansen was awarded the Nobel Peace Prize in 1922 for his work on behalf of Armenian and Russian refugees. This prize was also awarded in 1938 to the Nansen International Office, which had continued his work. Unfortunately, the Nansen Passport disappeared with the League of Nations.

Even with the disappearance of the Nansen Passport, one place remains as a motherland for all Armenians around the world – that place is the church. The church is much like a homeland for Armenians in the whole world. It is no coincidence that anywhere one sees an Armenian community, one also sees an Armenian Church, where the Lord is glorified and every member of the community feels welcomed, fed, satisfied, dressed, visited (Matt. 25:34-35). It is through God's church that the Armenian people retain their identity and struggle for recognition of the Armenian Genocide.

Every stateless and displaced person must find a landmark from which to fight for their own existence and identity. The Armenian people found it in their church, a place of communion and sharing, reassurance and hope. "We are always little believers among Armenians. The church, especially in the diaspora, is a little country," reflects Ara Aram S. Dzérounian in an interview to the French newspaper *Le Figaro* (24 April 2015). Another very strong testimony is shared by Albert Moscofian in the same newspaper: "My parents, they remained stateless. By dint of being called dirty foreigners, they had no desire to become French." The memories are very painful for this survivor: "I went to school in Ivry, it was before the war. At school, a teacher, whom I had asked to move me because I could not see well, replied that 'dirty foreigners stay at the bottom,' I have always heard that term. In the neighborhood, one family welcomed us, and they did not regard us as dirty foreigners. Later, Albert became a doctor. He still practices."

How many millions of destinies were and are broken like that? How many millions of doctors, lawyers, engineers, theologians, teachers, pastors are missing in the world? Because of the lack of recognition, of official papers, thousands of people are waiting, they are waiting for their destiny. And the only place they can be at home is the house of God – the church. The house of God is the place of welcome and hospitality for Armenians; this should be the case for every Christian. Those who believe in him receive "in his name," his envoys (John 13:20) and also all men, even the most humble (Luke 9:48), they see in any stranger not only an "angel" sent by the Lord (Gen. 19:1ff), but the Lord himself (Matt. 10:40).

That is why, far from treating the aliens as debtors (Eccles. 29:24-28), or distrusting (Eccles. 11:34) and murmuring against them (1 Pet. 4:9), we need to welcome those who cannot pay back the services they benefit from: "But when you give a banquet, invite the poor, the crippled, the lame, and the blind" (Luke 14:13). Every Christian (1 Tim. 3:2) must see in the person who knocks on the door God's son from his Father to fill them and welcome them home: "Listen! I am standing at the door, knocking; if you hear my voice and open the door, I will come in to you and eat with you, and you with me" (Rev. 3:20). And these divine guests in turn enter the home as a child of the house (John 14:2f; Eph. 2:19). Blessed are vigilant servants who will open the door to the Master, especially at the second coming! Reversing roles and manifesting the mystery of hospitality, it is he who will serve at table (Luke 12:37); it is he who will share his meal.

CHAPTER 4

FROM CLIMATE-UPROOTED PEOPLE TO PILGRIMS: NOAH AND THE FLOOD (GEN. 6-9)

GUILLERMO KERBER

These are the descendants of Noah. Noah was a righteous man, blameless in his generation; Noah walked with God. [10] And Noah had three sons, Shem, Ham, and Japheth.[11] Now the earth was corrupt in God's sight, and the earth was filled with violence. [12] And God saw that the earth was corrupt; for all flesh had corrupted its ways upon the earth. [13] And God said to Noah, "I have determined to make an end of all flesh, for the earth is filled with violence because of them; now I am going to destroy them along with the earth. [14] Make yourself an ark of cypress[a] wood; make rooms in the ark, and cover it inside and out with pitch. [15] This is how you are to make it: the length of the ark three hundred cubits, its width fifty cubits, and its height thirty cubits. [16] Make a roof[b] for the ark, and finish it to a cubit above; and put the door of the ark in its side; make it with lower, second, and third decks. [17] For my part, I am going to bring a flood of waters on the earth, to destroy from under heaven all flesh in which is the breath of life; everything that is on the earth shall die. [18] But I will establish my covenant with you; and you shall come into the ark, you, your sons, your wife, and your sons' wives with you. [19] And of every living thing, of all flesh, you shall bring two of every kind into the ark, to keep them alive with you; they shall be male and female. [20] Of the birds according to their kinds, and of the animals according to their kinds, of every creeping thing of the ground according to its kind, two of every kind shall come in to you, to keep them alive. [21] Also take with you every kind of food that is eaten, and store it up; and it shall serve as food for you and for them." [22] Noah did this; he did all that God commanded him.

7 Then the Lord said to Noah, "Go into the ark, you and all your household, for I have seen that you alone are righteous before me in this generation. [2] Take with you seven pairs of all clean animals, the male and its mate; and a pair of the animals that are not clean, the male and its mate; [3] and seven pairs of the birds of the air also, male and female, to keep their kind alive on the face of all the earth. [4] For in seven days I will send rain on the earth for forty days and forty nights; and every living thing that I have made I will blot out from the face of the ground." [5] And Noah did all that the Lord had commanded him. [6] Noah was six hundred years old when the flood of waters came on the earth. [7] And Noah with his sons and his wife and his sons' wives went into the ark to escape the waters of the flood. [8] Of clean animals, and of animals that are not clean, and of birds, and of everything that creeps on the ground, [9] two and two, male and female, went into the ark with Noah, as God had commanded Noah. [10] And after seven days the waters of the flood came on the earth. [11] In the six hundredth year of Noah's life, in the second month, on the seventeenth day of the month, on that day all the fountains of the great deep burst forth, and the windows of the heavens were opened. [12] The rain fell on the earth forty days and forty nights. [13] On the very same day Noah with his sons, Shem and Ham and Japheth, and Noah's wife and the three wives of his sons entered the ark, [14] they and every wild animal of every kind, and all domestic animals of every kind, and every creeping thing that creeps on the earth, and every bird of every kind—every bird, every winged creature. [15] They went into the ark with Noah, two and two of all flesh in which there was the breath of life. [16] And those that entered, male and female of all flesh, went in as God had commanded him; and the Lord shut him in. [17] The flood continued forty days on the earth; and the waters increased, and bore up the ark, and it rose high above the earth. ¹⁸ *The waters swelled and increased greatly on the earth; and the ark floated on the face of the waters.* ¹⁹ *The waters swelled so mightily on the earth that all the high mountains under the whole heaven were covered;* ²⁰ *the waters swelled above the mountains, covering them fifteen cubits deep.* ²¹ *And all flesh died that moved on the earth, birds, domestic animals, wild animals, all swarming creatures that swarm on the earth, and all human beings;* ²² *everything on dry land in whose nostrils was the breath of life died.* ²³ *He blotted out every living thing that was on the face of the ground, human beings and animals and creeping things and birds of the air; they were blotted out from the earth. Only Noah was left, and those that were with him in the ark.* ²⁴ *And the waters swelled on the earth for one hundred fifty days.*

8 But God remembered Noah and all the wild animals and all the domestic animals that were with him in the ark. And God made a wind blow over the earth, and the waters subsided; ² *the fountains of the deep and the windows of the heavens were closed, the rain from the heavens was restrained,* ³ *and the waters gradually receded from the earth. At the end of one hundred fifty days the waters had abated;* ⁴ *and in the seventh month, on the seventeenth day of the month, the ark came to rest on the mountains of Ararat.* ⁵ *The waters continued to abate until the tenth month; in the tenth month, on the first day of the month, the tops of the mountains appeared.* ⁶ *At the end of forty days Noah opened the window of the ark that he had made* ⁷ *and sent out the raven; and it went to and fro until the waters were dried up from the earth.* ⁸ *Then he sent out the dove from him, to see if the waters had subsided from the face of the ground;* ⁹ *but the dove found no place to set its foot, and it returned to him to the ark, for the waters were still on the face of the whole earth. So he put out his hand and took it and brought it into the ark with him.* ¹⁰ *He waited another seven days, and again he sent out the dove from the ark;* ¹¹ *and the dove came back to him in the evening, and there in its beak was a freshly plucked olive leaf; so Noah knew that the waters had subsided from the earth.* ¹² *Then he waited another seven days, and sent out the dove; and it did not return to him any more.* ¹³ *In the six hundred first year, in* *the first month, on the first day of the month, the waters were dried up from the earth; and Noah removed the covering of the ark, and looked, and saw that the face of the ground was drying. ¹⁴ In the second month, on the twenty-seventh day of the month, the earth was dry. ¹⁵ Then God said to Noah, ¹⁶ "Go out of the ark, you and your wife, and your sons and your sons' wives with you. ¹⁷ Bring out with you every living thing that is with you of all flesh—birds and animals and every creeping thing that creeps on the earth—so that they may abound on the earth, and be fruitful and multiply on the earth." ¹⁸ So Noah went out with his sons and his wife and his sons' wives. ¹⁹ And every animal, every creeping thing, and every bird, everything that moves on the earth, went out of the ark by families. ²⁰ Then Noah built an altar to the Lord, and took of every clean animal and of every clean bird, and offered burnt offerings on the altar. ²¹ And when the Lord smelled the pleasing odor, the Lord said in his heart, "I will never again curse the ground because of humankind, for the inclination of the human heart is evil from youth; nor will I ever again destroy every living creature as I have done.*

²² As long as the earth endures,
seedtime and harvest, cold and heat,
summer and winter, day and night,
shall not cease."

9 God blessed Noah and his sons, and said to them, "Be fruitful and multiply, and fill the earth. ² The fear and dread of you shall rest on every animal of the earth, and on every bird of the air, on everything that creeps on the ground, and on all the fish of the sea; into your hand they are delivered. ³ Every moving thing that lives shall be food for you; and just as I gave you the green plants, I give you everything. ⁴ Only, you shall not eat flesh with its life, that is, its blood. ⁵ For your own lifeblood I will surely require a reckoning: from every animal I will require it and from human beings, each one for the blood of another, I will require a reckoning for human life.

⁶ Whoever sheds the blood of a human,
by a human shall that person's blood be shed;
for in his own image
God made humankind.

⁷ And you, be fruitful and multiply, abound on the earth and multiply in it."
⁸ Then God said to Noah and to his sons with him, ⁹ "As for me, I am establishing my covenant with you and your descendants after you, ¹⁰ and with every living creature that is with you, the birds, the domestic animals, and every animal of the earth with you, as many as came out of the ark.[c] ¹¹ I establish my covenant with you, that never again shall all flesh be cut off by the waters of a flood, and never again shall there be a flood to destroy the earth." ¹² God said, "This is the sign of the covenant that I make between me and you and every living creature that is with you, for all future generations: ¹³ I have set my bow in the clouds, and it shall be a sign of the covenant between me and the earth. ¹⁴ When I bring clouds over the earth and the bow is seen in the clouds, ¹⁵ I will remember my covenant that is between me and you and every living creature of all flesh; and the waters shall never again become a flood to destroy all flesh. ¹⁶ When the bow is in the clouds, I will see it and remember the everlasting covenant between God and every living creature of all flesh that is on the earth." ¹⁷ God said to Noah, "This is the sign of the covenant that I have established between me and all flesh that is on the earth." (Gen. 6:9–9:17)

Some years ago, when I was participating at a conference on climate displacement organized by the Pacific Conference of Churches in Fiji, a pastor from Tuvalu stood up at the beginning of the conference and said: "I don't believe in climate change. God told Noah after the flood that there would be no other flood and that the rainbow was the symbol of the new covenant God was doing with his people." Another pastor, from the same church in Tuvalu responded: "I have seen the corals bleaching, the salinization of our drinking water sources, the rise of sea level. We need to prepare our people to deal with climate change."

This dialogue struck me and showed me how Bible stories have, indeed, various interpretations for Christians, even from the same church and community. Several times since then over the years I have shared some reflections on this story,[1] as it conveys, I believe, a critical message for the challenge of climate-induced displacement, which, according to experts, might be a cause of statelessness in the coming decades.

The animals, the flood, the rainbow

The story of Noah and the flood is, perhaps, one of the most well-known stories in the Bible. It would be interesting to check, before going to the text itself, what we remember from the story. What are the images that come to mind?

I have some images that come immediately: the whole earth covered by the waters; the ark to which a pair of every kind of animal is brought, together with Noah's family; the dove sent from the ark and coming back with an olive branch of olive tree.

The story of Noah is narrated in various chapters of the book of Genesis. It is part of what is called the "book of the origins" in the first book of the Bible. Before the stories of the Patriarchs, which start with Abraham in chapter 12, the book narrates the origins of the earth and of humankind. The story of Noah and the flood appears in chapters 6 to 9.

It is interesting to note that stories about a flood or deluge covering the earth are part of religious and spiritual traditions starting with the epic of Gilgamesh, from Babylon (approximately 2100 BCE) to stories in China, Hawaii, Scandinavia, Central, and North and South America. The flood as punishment, cleansing of the earth, a new beginning are common in various of these narratives.

The biblical story's contents unfold as follows:

---

1. See for example Guillermo Kerber, "Noah: An Uprooted Pilgrim," *Seven Weeks for Water 2011: Biblical Reflections on Water and Just Peace*, Ecumenical Water Network (Geneva: WCC Publications, 2011), 14-15.

- The Lord sees how great the wickedness of the human race had become on the earth, and that "every inclination of the thoughts of their hearts was only evil continually" (Gen. 6:5).

- God calls Noah to build the ark, to bring into it his family and a pair of all living creatures.

- Then the floodwaters come to earth for 40 days.

- When the waters recede, after 150 days, those in the ark are the only ones who have survived.

- When they come out of the ark, a new covenant is established between God and the whole creation with the solemn promise – never again will there be a flood to destroy the earth (Gen. 9:8).

- And a rainbow is the sign of the everlasting covenant between God and all living creatures (Gen. 9:16).

Displaced by climate

Although today we don't see a single flood covering the whole earth, the increase of frequency and intensity of rains, hurricanes, and cyclones have produced devastating floods across the earth. Millions of people have been displaced in Bangladesh, the Caribbean, the Americas, Australia, and Europe. The increase of flooding is one of the consequences of human-induced climate change. Today, it is not God who provokes the flood, as in the Noah story, but rather human beings who are provoking the destructive flooding with their behaviour toward the earth and its creatures.

As in Noah's story, the whole creation is being affected. St Paul in Romans talked about the groaning of creation (Rom. 8:22). Biodiversity is dramatically decreasing as a result of the current development pattern, which follows the "mantra" of unlimited economic growth and man's insatiable greed. Monocultures, deforestation, pollution, increase of ocean temperatures and the extension of megacities are dramatically affecting ecosystems and provoking the destruction of species.

Together with the millions of people displaced because of floods, tens of thousands are being displaced in the Great Lakes and Horn of Africa regions because of the change in rainfall patterns that alters the cycle of planting and harvesting, preventing people from having access to food. At the same time, global warming has provoked the rise of sea water leading to the need for some populations to resettle. This has been the case already for the inhabitants of the Carteret Islands, who had to be moved to Bougainville in Papua New Guinea, and for the coastal villages in Fiji, which were relocated at higher altitudes in the country.

Other low-lying islands states are currently holding crucial negotiations to resettle their populations, such as the Maldives in the Indian Ocean or Tuvalu and Kiribati in the Pacific. As one author asks, "With the absence of physical territory, will the nationals of these countries be considered stateless? There are already hundreds of climate-displaced persons coming from these low-lying islands. Do they risk becoming stateless when their island completely disappears?"[2]

These and other similar questions were the basis for the two conferences on climate refugees organized by the World Council of Churches (WCC) together with the Pacific Conference of Churches and Bread for the World in 2010 and 2012. These conferences aimed at deepening the understanding of the issue in consultation with victims, church representatives, academics, and politicians in order to enhance the protection of climate-induced displaced persons and identify further ways to bridge the gaps in the international protection system. [3]

Coming back to our opening dialogue, in the Pacific the salinization of fresh water and the bleaching of corals, referred to by the pastor in Tuvalu, have already affected fauna and flora in these fragile ecosystems. The severe drought in 2011 that affected Tuvalu together with the salinization of

2. Semegnish Asfaw, *The Invisible among Us: Hidden, Forgotten, Stateless* (Geneva: WCC Publicaitions, 2016), 12.

3. The report of the two consultations has been published as Sophia Wirsching, Peter Emberson, and Guillermo Kerber (eds), *"Climate Refugees" People Displaced by Climate Change and the Role of the Churches* (Geneva: WCC Publications, 2013).

underground water made it necessary for them to get fresh water from New Zealand and Fiji, while other countries sent desalinization plants.

The resettlement of entire populations – the new reality of climate refugees and climate-displaced peoples – is the new face of uprooted people today and may be of stateless people in the near future.[4] Together with refugees, forced migrants, and internally displaced people, climate-related uprooted people are increasing today in various regions of the world.

Taking into account this reality, we need to recognize that Noah himself became an uprooted person. He is forced to leave his home, his land, and has to travel to an unknown destination. When elderly people in low-lying islands are asked about their future and whether they can see themselves living in another country, they say they would rather die than leave their land. For those of us living in cities, it is not easy to understand the bond that people who are forced to leave their homeland have with the land.

Yet at the same time, along with being an uprooted person, Noah is a pilgrim, because through his journey of his faith and hope, he is able to begin anew.

Climate-related displacement due to floods or rising sea levels does not occur without conflict. It is not easy for an uprooted community to adapt to a new situation, encountering a different culture, language, and environment. It is not easy either for a community, region, or country to deal with thousands of newcomers who are fleeing from disasters. More and more countries are closing their borders to poor migrants, while prejudices, xenophobia, and racism have increased because of these phenomena. The refugee crisis in Europe in 2015-2016 is a clear example. Strangers are rejected everywhere. Their rights – among them the rights to sustainable and decent life, education, health, adequate housing, and water and sanitation – are not respected. Embedding human rights into integration processes, stressing their universality and interconnectedness, remains a huge task in this area.[5]

The story of Noah is a call to conversion. If we look around we will easily find examples of the violent behaviour of human beings against

4. See ibid., 49-50.

5. See, e.g., the 2012 report to the UN General Assembly of the Special Rapporteur on the Human Rights of Migrants, thematic section on Climate Change and Migration, A/67/299.

neighbours and against the earth. Overconsumption, extreme poverty, a culture of waste, as pointed out by Pope Francis in the encyclical *Laudato si'*, are expressions of the same reality of greed, injustice and structural sin in our societies. The call for justice and peace expressed in the WCC's Pilgrimage of Justice and Peace is also a call to repentance, to convert (*metanoia*) our minds and behaviours, from destroying creation to caring for creation and welcoming the stranger in our midst – the refugee, the migrant, the stateless person. Caring for creation goes beyond human solidarity and love, it includes the whole creation as beautifully expressed in the Canticle of the Creatures of Saint Francis of Assisi. In other words, the story of Noah is a call to become pilgrims with him, his family, and all the animals in the ark, a symbol of our common home.

CHAPTER 5

THERE IS NOTHING NEW UNDER THE SUN: REFLECTIONS ON THE PENTATEUCH

SUZANNE MEMBE-MATALE

The Lord spoke to Moses in the tent of the meeting in the Desert of Sinai on the first day of the second month of the second year after the Israelites came out of Egypt. He said: "Take a census of the whole Israelite community by their clans and families, listing every man by name, one by one. You and Aaron are to count according to their divisions all the men in Israel who are twenty years old or more and able to serve in the army. (Lev. 1:1-3)

Lineage and birth registration in the Hebrew Bible

The Old Testament books, in my view, begin with a very orderly and deliberate approach regarding the people's organization and planning for the future of that first generation.[1] The book of Genesis records two beautiful creation stories. In relation to the subject at hand is the history of the descendants of Adam and Eve in Genesis 4 and 5. Genesis 5, verses 1-2, records: "This is the list of the descendants of Adam. When God created humankind, he made them in the likeness of God. Male and female he created them, and he blessed them and named them Humankind." If one reads the whole chapter, one will find a whole registration of births from Adam to Noah. Each

---

1. This article was presented as a morning reflection at the WCC Regional Workshop on Birth Registration and Gender Discriminatory Nationality Laws in Africa Addis-Ababa, Ethiopia, 11-13 May 2016.

birth was recorded. In the same chapter there is a record of how long they lived and when their children were born. In other words, there was serious attention to lineage and even registration in early Israel.

Actually, one could say that the registration process begins in chapter 4 when Adam and Eve start to have their children. The fact that in the narrative they were recorded by name is an indication of the importance of naming and remembering people by name in the Hebrew tradition. Adam and Eve's children were Abel, Cain, and then later on Seth, after the death of Abel. Most of the narratives in the book of Genesis, in between events, rigorously record births and deaths of people. All these records suggest to us that no one was left undocumented or "stateless." One could trace lineage and genealogy all the way back to the creation of the world. I imagine that even girl children were registered but not counted in the numbers, as was always the case and still is in some cases of gender discrimination, where girls and women are disregarded. Unfortunately women were only named as wives and sisters. What is certain, at least for narrative purposes, is that people were recorded according to their families, clans, and nations. When I was studying theology, one of my lecturers tried to convince us that when the Bible refers to men, it also includes women. This notion remains debatable.

The second book of the Pentateuch, Exodus, gives an account of God's plan to have the Israelites freed from bondage – "Let my people go." It is quite interesting that the records of births and deaths continued. I would like to pick up the story of the birth of Moses in Egypt as an example. The story of Moses' birth is very dramatic; however, the point I want to make is that while Moses grew up in the palace as a foster child, his real and original identity was not deleted and forgotten. Someone had kept a record of his origins, and it came to pass that at some point he reconnected with his clan, tribe, and family. Eventually he became the "saviour" of the Israelites who had been in bondage for so long, taking them out of Egypt (the house of bondage) to the promised land under God's guidance. Exodus states, "The following are the heads of their ancestral houses" (Ex. 6:14). In this genealogy, Moses and Aaron are recorded as being descendants of the clan of Levites and they are listed according to their family groups. Again the point here is that birth registration at that time was not a mere academic exercise, at least in the narrator's mind. Its importance goes beyond just obtaining and possessing a document. Registration of people is a very useful tool: first of all, as a way of confidence building, in that one belongs to a certain tribe, clan or family. More importantly, it allows people to claim their ancestral inheritance and pride – in some cases of belonging to people who made great strides in their contributions to humanity. This gives energy to people to strive toward the future with hope, knowing that they are from a good background. Moses was able to claim his place in the family and clan. He was able to start a journey to the promised land together with his people. Because of the registers that God insisted on, Moses did not arrive as a stateless stranger in a foreign land. The Israelites were able to leave a country that was not theirs; they were anxious to go home, to a place they could call their own.

The third book in the Bible, Leviticus, details the codes of conduct of the people and the various sanctions to be applied if those codes were violated by the freed people. It describes the dress code and prescribes ordination robes and colours. Even though the matter of registration is not prominent in this book, one can conclude, based on the registration by clan, that the clan of Levites was chosen for priesthood. God instructs Moses, "Take Aaron and his sons with him, the vestments, the anointing oil, the bull of sin offering, the two rams, and the basket of unleavened bread" (Lev. 8:2). This call to Aaron and his children for ordination must have came from their being set upon according to God's instruction to register people according to families, clans and tribes for specific functions or tasks. In today's interpretation, one would say that God used the records and registration statistics gathered according in the books of Genesis and Exodus for use along the journey.

Then comes the book of Numbers. The book of Numbers was written to the people of Israel to remind them to document their journey to the promised land, but it also reminds all future readers of the Bible that God is with us as we journey through the world or universe that he created. The book is careful to instruct them to move with their clans, families, and tribes in order to stay close to one another. God speaks warmly but strongly about the importance of family because happy families make a better society. Instructions abound in the scripture of how this is done – making a happy family.

We note from the Book of Numbers that the instructions to Moses asking him to register – or to take a census of people – by tribe, family, and clan, one by one, according to their divisions comes from God's mouth. They were also to register every male who was one month and older (birth registration). This event is recorded in the book of Numbers as follows:

> *Then the Lord spoke to Moses in the wilderness of Sinai, saying: Enroll the Levites by ancestral houses and by clans. You shall enroll every male from a month old and upward. So Moses enrolled them according to the word of the Lord, as he was commanded. The following were the sons of Levi, by their names: Gershon, Kohath, and Merari. These are the names of the sons of Gershon by their clans: Libni and Shimei. The sons of Kohath by their clans: Amram, Izhar, Hebron, and Uzziel. The sons of Merari by their clans: Mahli and Mushi. These are the clans of the Levites, by their ancestral houses. (Num. 3:14-20)*

The records above are reminiscent of the birth certificates of today, which require, at least in my country, that parents provide information related to the place and date of birth of the child, the full names of parents, and the full given names of the child. Certified copies of the parents' national registration/identification cards would be attached to the application for registration of birth, which would give details about the parents' original place of birth and their ancestors: for example, the name of the village, the name of the chief, the tribe or tribes of the parents, the districts, and the provinces. With such a record, a person can be traced back to their ancestors going back generations.

We also note from the book of Numbers that this registration was also a way of determining people capable of defending the community, determining their military strength but also their ability to contribute to the well-being of their communities. A census or count of the people was needed as a tool to prepare them for future tasks. For instance, in chapter 3 of the book of Numbers, Gershom's descendants are assigned the area to the west of the tabernacle for their camp. Their responsibility was to care for the tabernacle – its layers of coverings, its entry curtains – as well as other assignments. Kohath's descendants were assigned the area to the south of the tabernacle, and were responsible for the ark, the table, the lampstand, the altars. The descendants of Merari were assigned the area to the north of the tabernacle for their camp, and were responsible for the frames supporting the tabernacle, the cross-bars, the pillars, the bases, and all the equipment related to their use. The areas to the east in front of the tabernacle toward the sunrise were reserved for the tents of Moses and Aaron and his sons, who had final responsibility for the sanctuary on behalf of the people of Israel.

Although one cannot be sure of the historical reliability of these narratives, they are broadly indicative of the religious and cultural concerns of the Hebrew people. Reading through this story, one cannot help but deduce that the God we serve is a very organized God. My lesson from this allocation of land by family, assignment of responsibility, and appointment of leadership is that census-gathering is a good thing. It is a powerful analogy of what registration of births in today's time can do, all things being equal. We have noted how developed countries assign and distribute work and wealth to their nationals. They depend on birth registration statistics to plan the future, to anticipate the challenges and respond to those challenges even before they occur.

The first few chapters in the book of Numbers describe how the census was also used to create boundaries between families and clans for the purposes of distributing land (wealth) equitably, so that no one was left behind or left with nothing. This same census also helped in the organizational planning and governance of their new community.

It is also important to note that in those days, registration of people was important generally for the purpose of military command and to ensure that everyone paid taxes to the authorities. While it may not be explicit in the texts referred to, we can infer in some cases that the purpose of census-taking was to increase pride and self-reliance. It may also have been to involve everyone in self-preservation and protection.

The family theme also comes out strongly in the process of registration. The Bible instructs to count them by tribe and by family; I believe this was important for succession purposes and wealth distribution. In those days, the names of families and clans were very important. A name told something about the character of a person. Each family or each clan was given a specific task to do, and these tasks ran in the family for centuries.

The book of 2 Chronicles 2:17-18 reveals that they were careful to register foreigners among them in Israel. Foreigners were assigned specific roles to keep them working, and also so that they could contribute to the sustaining the community. They were recognized as not being natives, but still were to be registered as foreigners who would go back to their ancestral land at some point. We also read in Ezra 2 that a complete census of people was recorded in the time of Nehemiah after the return of the exiles from Babylon to Jerusalem.

Lineage in the New Testament

In the New Testament, the Gospel of Luke 2:1-5 also refers to a decree by Augustus that all people return to their ancestral home throughout the Roman Empire. Jesus' parents hearkened to the call and went for registration. Since Jesus was born in his parents' ancestral home, he was likely also registered. Jesus' own genealogy is recorded from the beginning to the end. You find the record of Jesus' ancestors in Matthew 1, stretching from Abraham to Isaac, to Jacob and many others in between, and passing on to Jesse the father of King David, on to Solomon, then all the way to Joseph the husband of Mary, the mother of Jesus, who is called the Messiah. About fourteen generations were recorded from Abraham to King David, fourteen generations from David's time to the Babylonian exile, and fourteen generations from the Babylonian exile to the Messiah. This genealogy has very explicit purposes for Matthew's narrative and his framing of Jesus' identity as a descendant of David and in the messianic line, but it also indicates the importance in ancient culture generally of ancestry and the roots of one's identity.

A measure of human dignity: the roles of governments and churches

While my exposition is not necessarily on the specific reasons for the decrees of asking people to go to register, the important point is that statistics are a critical and vital component in any nation's development. The other point that I am trying to make from the above biblical writings is that registration of people by tribe, clan, family, and nation is not a new phenomenon. It has always been important that people made in God's image be accounted for, wherever they are, whatever they do, and wherever they go. The bottom line is that registration is vital in our lives. No one should be stateless. Each individual should be connected by bloodline, by clan, by family. We have already established above how important family is. We witness, we read, and we hear how adopted children, when they grow up, have a longing and hunger to find their birth parents. It takes, for some, a whole lifetime to seek for their roots. There is something in-built in all human being that wills them to return to the roots of their parents. It is biblical that we stay close to our kith and kin. My conclusion is that birth registration is also a spiritual issue. It is commonly said that no matter how poor or rich, "home is sweet home." There is something in us as human beings that thirsts for "home" before the spirit or soul rests. Even when people die, their wish is to be taken home, to be interred in their home soil – in the land of their ancestors. This is only possible if one has been registered as a national of his or her homeland.

In today's world, which is full of conflicts leading to displacement and pushing many people to become refugees, anyone without documentation, as many people are today, risks becoming invisible. Officially they do not exist, and such people are prone to terrible abuses in their nomadic status. In many parts of the world today, especially on the African continent, many children are never registered at birth. The risk, in addition to being invisible, is that they cannot get a national identity card to prove they are nationals of a country, they cannot get a passport to travel as they wish, and they cannot pursue a higher education or their preferred careers, as identity cards and proof of nationality are usually required. Stateless people cannot be employed normally, and they lose out on many rights and benefits due to them that are provided by their countries of birth. If they are displaced, they also are prone to too many abuses (modern slavery, sexual abuse, child labour, poor housing) and they have no recourse to justice.

God their Creator is looking down on the neglect of his people and shedding tears for this state of affairs in his world. Jesus Christ, during his mission on earth, in his practical, clear, and matter of fact fashion, declared, "'I came that they may have life, and have it abundantly" (John 10:10). And yet we find people who are charged with the responsibility to take care of his creation doing the exact opposite of his intentions and wishes – that is, "to steal and kill and destroy."

Lessons learned: Here is what I take from reflecting on the narratives:

1. That there is nothing new under the sun. God is the Creator of the heavens and the earth and all that is within it, therefore it is very important to him that his creation, human beings, made in his image, must be accounted for at all times because we carry his image with a full mandate to care for one another and to be our sister's and brother's keeper. This can also be possible if all people are registered, accounted for, and given their dignity, so that no one in the world remains stateless, without nationality, or undocumented.

Statelessness is not of God. The Bible has given us many examples of the importance of registration and census.

2. In order to achieve God's mission for dignity for all, numbers help in planning for protection and the well-being of all people; according to John 10:10, he came so that well might have life and have it abundantly. A good nation is one that keeps accounts of all people being born daily in their precincts to ensure that they are accompanied in their journey in the world from birth to death.

3. Registration of births is important in that it notifies authorities about the existence of another human being, who must be careful to consider the need for equitable distribution of resources, just as God instructed Moses to count the people and to divide the land according to the size of the families or clans.

4. I am convinced that God's plan is for people to have protection of inheritance and continuation of ancestry. We have an example in the biblical narratives of the importance of ancestral records and birth registration. We have learned from their experiences, both good and bad.

5. Clans and families are very important to all of us. It explains many things about who we are. It gives us a sense of belonging and the comfort that we are not alone in the world.

6. Registration, as it has throughout history, provides us with permanent records of our existence.

The global campaign to encourage registration of births has many advantages that lead – or should I say, "that should lead" – to justice and fairness for all. It helps to plan ahead for the future and good governance of the nations with regard to access to health care, education, protection of nations, protection of people, maintenance of family legacies, and permanent records of existence. It has been proven that through these records, families have been reunited. This will ensure that no one remains stateless.

Churches around the world clearly should embrace promoting the campaign for birth registration, as it is within their mandate to help secure the dignity of all human beings through their already established structures, using the power of the pulpit.

In certain countries, like mine, birth registration is not an issue that the government appears to take seriously. Provision of this important service to its citizen has not been prioritized. Many people, especially in rural areas, remain undocumented. This creates the potential in the event of conflict for many people to become stateless with no one to claim them. This state of affairs is contrary to the plan and design of God for all God's people. The Bible clearly states that people must be registered, accounted for, and secure in knowing that they have a country, a nation, a family, a clan, and a place to call home – a place where they can freely enjoy their God-given rights without fear of displacement.

CHAPTER 6

SECURITY, SURVIVAL, AND SEX IN THE BOOK OF RUTH

EVELYN L. PARKER

1⁶Then she started to return with her daughters-in-law from the country of Moab, for she had heard in the country of Moab that the Lord had considered his people and given them food. ⁷So she set out from the place where she had been living, she and her two daughters-in-law, and they went on their way to go back to the land of Judah. ⁸But Naomi said to her two daughters-in-law, "Go back each of you to your mother's house. May the Lord deal kindly with you, as you have dealt with the dead and with me. ⁹The Lord grant that you may find security, each of you in the house of your husband." The she kissed them, and they wept aloud. ¹⁰They said to her, "No, we will return with you to your people." ¹¹But Naomi said, "Turn back, my daughters, why will you go with me? Do I still have sons in my womb that they may become your husbands? ¹² Turn back, my daughters, go your way, for I am too old to have a husband. Even if I thought there was hope for me, even if I should have a husband tonight and bear sons, ¹³would you then wait until they were grown? Would you then refrain from marrying? No, my daughters, it has been far more bitter for me than for you, because the hand of the Lord has turned against me." ¹⁴Then they wept aloud again. Orpah kissed her mother-in-law, but Ruth clung to her. ¹⁵So she said, "See, your sister-in-law has gone back to her people and to her gods; return after your sister-in-law."

2¹Now Naomi had a kinsman on her husband's side a prominent rich man, of the family of Elimelech, whose name was Boaz. ²And Ruth the Moabite said to Naomi, "Let me go to the field and glean among the ears of grain, behind someone in whose sight I may find favor." She said to her "Go, my daughter."...

¹⁰Then she fell prostrate, with her face to the ground, and said to him, "Why have I found favor in your sight, that you should take notice of me, when I am a foreigner?"...

3¹Naomi her mother-in-law said to her, "My daughter, I need to seek some security for you, so that it may be well with you. ²Now here is our kinsman Boaz, with whose young women you have been working. See, he is winnowing barley tonight at the threshing floor. ³Now wash and anoint yourself and put on your best clothes and go down to the threshing floor; but do not make yourself known to the man until he has finished eating and drinking. ⁴When he lies down, observe the place where he lies; then go and uncover his feet and lie down; and he will tell you what to do." ⁵She said to her, "All that you tell me I will do." (Ruth 1:6-15; 2:1-2; 10, 3:1-5)

The book of Ruth is often read from the perspective of Naomi, the Ephrathites woman from Bethlehem who, at the onset of the story, loses her husband Elimelech and two sons, Mahlon and Chilion. She is left in a patriarchal world where having a husband and male children can be a matter of life or death. Another perspective is the faithfulness that Ruth, the character for whom the book is named, shows to her mother-in-law Naomi after her husband Chilion dies. How can we understand the story of Ruth – a poor, widowed foreign woman – from the perspective of a woman at risk of dehumanization in a patriarchal society? In a similar manner, stateless women are vulnerable and at risk for dehumanization in a patriarchal world. Ruth's is a story that reveals the fragility of the security and welfare of women in a male-dominated and patriarchal society. Throughout the Bible, and specifically in the post-exilic period in which Ruth was written, women are not afforded security equal to that of men. Their only security from poverty and sexual exploitation is marriage and having sons. If a woman is not married she is at risk for the basic human needs of food and shelter, as well as vulnerable to other dehumanizing situations. In a patriarchal society, men have authority over every aspect of women's existence, oppressing and subordinating them through political, economic, social, sexual, and religious practices and institutions. Economically, an unmarried woman is subject to poverty and must struggle to get basic necessities. Examples of men's sexual domination of women include sexual coercion of women who need money or shelter for herself and her children. Rape, either within or outside of marriage, is a form of sexual domination. If a woman does not mutually consent to sexual relations with a man, then she is raped. The rape of Tamar in 2 Samuel 13 is an example of sexual domination in the Hebrew Bible. Such male domination results in the difficulty of women flourishing and maintaining human dignity.

According to the *Women's Bible Commentary*, Ruth is the only book in the biblical canon to be named after a foreign woman. Ruth is a Moabite heroine whose name means friend or companion. The extensive foregrounding of women's experiences and voices in this ancient story has led some scholars to argue that it may have had a female author, even though there is no proof for such an authorship. Nevertheless, the noticeable presence of women invites those who read Ruth to consider the subversive approach to patriarchy. As mentioned above, the book of Ruth is situated in the postexilic period and is perhaps a rebuttal to policies against inter-ethnic marriages found in Ezra and Nehemiah.

Ruth in an insecure world

The story begins with the head of the household, Elimelech, dying after relocating his wife and two sons to Moab because of a famine in Judah (Ruth 1:1-3). Even though Elimelech, who had power to give security for his family, is gone, his widow Naomi still has their two sons to support and provide for her. The sons marry Orpah and Ruth, foreign women from the land of Moab, who also obtain the revered status of married women (Ruth 1:4). In a patriarchal society, due to cultural expectations, men have access to resources and networks with other men that guarantee they can provide for their families. Orpah and Ruth are married for about ten years to Mahlon and Chilion, respectively, yet the couples remain childless. If they had had children, then they would have had a fifty percent chance of having male children to secure their future as honored women. Nevertheless, the young women are childless. Then Mahlon and Chilion die (Ruth 1:5) leaving Orpah and Ruth widowed and childless, the most extreme state of insecurity and vulnerability for women in that time period. Naomi as well is now not only a widow but also childless. All three women are thus poor, widowed, and childless. They are at high risk of being exploited and in danger of losing their lives because there are no men to give them security.

However, Naomi has the option of going back to her country of Judah and the city of Bethlehem where she has a better chance of gaining the security she needs to live out the rest of her days as a widowed woman. Word has come all the way from Judah to Moab that the famine is over and her God, the God of Abraham, Isaac, and Jacob the Patriarchs, has given the people food. Hearing this, she plans to return with her daughters-in-law from the country of Moab (Ruth 1:6); but she changes her mind and suggests that returning to their biological mothers will bring them the security she cannot provide as a poor widow without male children: "The Lord grant that you may find security, each of you in the house of your husband." Naomi invokes a blessing that the Lord "deals kindly" with the young women to marry again and have sons. The text suggests Naomi's realization that Orpah's and Ruth's likelihood of finding security – that is, a husband – in their native country of Moab is greater than it would be in Judah, where they will be not only foreign women, but Moabites. Foreign women are least likely to find a husband, especially if they are from the country of Moab.

Moab was a land east of the Dead Sea, a country and people of Transjordania. The land was a fertile plateau where farmers could plant and grow plenty of food with little concern about famine, unlike Judah, where the lack of food was the reason that Elimelech sought food security for his wife and sons in the fertile land of Moab. However, given the origin of the Moabites,

Moab was the least likely place for a Jewish family to choose to go. Moabites were descendants of Lot's son, Moab, who born from an incestuous relationship with his elder daughter after they fled from Sodom, which was destroyed by an earthquake and a volcanic eruption (Gen. 19). Scholars indicate that descendants of Abraham despised descendants of his nephew Lot because of this history. The Israelites had instruction from Yahweh through Moses not to allow Moabites, down to the tenth generation, to be admitted into the Assembly of God (Deut. 23:3). However, despite the incestuous heritage of the Moabites and Yahweh's edict, Elimelech chose this people and their land when he needed to secure food for his family.

Ruth 1:4b indicates that Elimelech, Naomi, Mahlon, and Chilion were foreigners in the land of Moab for "about ten years." From Naomi's words and actions toward Orpah and Ruth, it seems that the Moabites received Naomi and her family kindly while she was a foreigner. The hospitality of the Moabites allowed the Jewish family to continue their cultural and religious practices. Also, Naomi's sons engaged in interracial marriage, in contrast to the exclusionary policies of Ezra and Nehemiah and the forced dissolution of foreign marriages (Ezra 9-10 and Neh. 13).

Ruth 1:10-11 describes the debate between Naomi and her daughters-in-law over her rational choice of their returning to their Moabite mothers hoping that they will find new husbands of Moabite ancestry to provide them with security. With the exchange of kisses and loud weeping of Orpah and Ruth, Naomi explains what is at stake as poor, childless, foreign widowed Moabite women in Judah and her own status of an old widowed childless woman. Even if Naomi found a husband at that very moment, she explains, she would not be able to bear sons for them to marry. And even if she could, Orpah and Ruth would be too old to have sons of their own from Naomi's second set of male children: "Even if I thought there was hope for me, even if I should have a husband tonight and bear sons, would you then wait until they were grown? Would you then refrain from marrying? No, my daughters" (Ruth 1:13). She laments that the Lord whom she serves has turned against her and now life is "far more bitter" without the security of a husband.

Orpah is convinced that she should return to her mother in Moab, but Ruth is not. Ruth clings to Naomi and refuses to return to Moab, despite the potential insecurity and unknown peril she may face. In verses 16-17, Ruth declares that she will adopt Naomi's lodging, people, and God as her own, even until death. And unlike the custom of the time and region, Ruth is willing to be buried in a foreign country. Lastly, Ruth's dramatic petition to Naomi reflects the ultimate risk-taking when she states, "May the Lord do thus and so to me, and more as well, if even death parts me from you!" (Ruth1:17b). Clearly, Ruth is willing to risk even her life to follow Naomi. Thus, Ruth accompanies Naomi to Bethlehem leaving all possibility and potential for security as a woman in a patriarchal world behind. They arrive in Bethlehem at the beginning of the barley harvest (Ruth 1:22b).

Ruth's search for security and food

Once settled, the task for the two women is to survive, specifically to secure food. Like a scene in a play, chapter 2 opens with dialogue between Ruth and Naomi strategizing about how to obtain food, which is at the intersection of survival and sexuality. Naomi agrees with Ruth that she should find grain for them to eat and to do it in a place where she can attract the attention of a rich man: "Let me go to the field and glean among the ears of grain, behind someone in whose sight I may find favor" (Ruth 2:2). The plot to catch a man is far from innocent, for this suggests Ruth wants to attract a certain man who will give her and Naomi security. The target is Naomi's kinsman Boaz, a prominent rich relative of her deceased husband Elimelech. According to Jewish law, a close relative of the deceased husband should take the Jewish widow into his home if there were no sons to care for her. The text suggests that such familial practices are not automatic, but we learn in chapter 3 that Boaz is not the designated relative to fulfill the Jewish tradition.

As Ruth is gleaning behind the reapers she probably inquires about Boaz's property and his usual time of arrival at his field. The plan works. She comes to the field owned by Boaz just in time for his arrival. He notices her and asks the servant: "To whom does this young woman belong?" (Ruth 2:5b). Ruth has found favor in Boaz's sight as she intended. The servant points out her identity. She is of a foreign nationality – a Moabite – despised by the Jewish community. But then the servant legitimizes her foreign status in the same sentence: "She is the Moabite *who came back with Naomi . . .*" (2:6). The servant points out Ruth's humility and tenacity in her pleading to glean after the reapers, and notes that she has gleaned from early in the morning without taking a rest (2:7). Boaz admonishes Ruth not to glean in any other fields but his and instructs her how to be safe from sexual harassment or potentially being raped (2:8-9). His interests are for her sexual safety and a foreshadowing of his own sexual engagements with her. Ruth, prostrate with her face to the ground, inquires why Boaz has found favor in her, a servant, who is also a foreigner (2:10). He replies that he knows she is not only a foreigner but a widow, a Moabite, and a hospitable and courageous young woman who sacrificed security in her homeland to accompany her mother-in-law. Indeed, Ruth did find favor with Boaz enough that he shares food with her at mealtime (2:14) and instructs the young male worker to provide opportunity for her to get grain even from the standing sheaves and the bundles (2:15-16). Boaz's favor in Ruth permits her to return to his fields and stay close to his servants/young women until they have finished all his harvest (2:21). When Ruth reports to Naomi, she is very pleased that Ruth has been favored by one of her "closest kin."

In chapter 3, once again, Naomi repeats the need for Ruth's security: "Naomi her mother-in-law said to her, 'My daughter, I need to seek some security for you, so that it may be well with you" (Ruth 3:1). But because it is the end of the harvest, gaining security now requires sexual work. Naomi lays out the plan for Ruth: when Boaz is winnowing barley on the threshing floor, Ruth is to wash, put on perfume and her best dress, and go down to the threshing floor. However, she is not to let Boaz know she is there until he has finished eating, drinking, and is in a contented mood. Then Ruth is to note where he lies down and go to him and "uncover his feet" (a euphemism for genitals) and lie down beside him (Ruth 3:4b). Ruth does all that Naomi instructs her to do. At midnight Boaz wakes up and is startled by Ruth's presence and asks, "Who are you"" (3:8-9). She identifies herself and asks that he spread his cloak over her for she is his next-of-kin. Boaz blesses Ruth, for "this last act of loyalty" (3:10) is better than that which she gave to Naomi. His words foreshadow the blessing that God will give Ruth, a son upon marriage to Boaz. Their son, Obed, will be the grandfather of David. Thus, while at the beginning of the story Ruth was a vulnerable foreign, poor, widowed, and childless young woman, her life is changed to that of a woman married to a rich man with whom she has a son. Ruth's blessing becomes Naomi's blessing, for she receives security from the presence of Boaz and adopts the new boy child as her own.

Although the story of Ruth is not about a woman who is stateless – that is, without nationality – Ruth's vulnerable state as a foreign, poor, widowed woman has relevance for stateless women. Women without nationality are also vulnerable because they are poor and without protection of the state or family members. Stateless women are not afforded the security of shelter, food, health care, voting privileges, and all other securities that come with nationality. As such, stateless women survive by any means possible and become vulnerable to the sex trade. A significant number of stateless women are trafficked for sex. The vulnerable state of stateless women is directly related to patriarchy and manifests itself in global society in many ways.

Patriarchy is at the centre of statelessness among women. Patriarchy affords men authority over every aspect of women's lives: politically, economically, socially, sexually, and religiously. Governments in over 60 countries shaped by patriarchy discriminate against women when it comes to acquisition, retention, or change of their nationality. In some countries women automatically lose their nationality when they marry a foreigner and may or may not acquire the husbands' nationality. Also, patriarchy is so egregious that women often automatically lose their nationality when their husbands lose or are deprived of their nationality.

CHAPTER 7

WALKING IN FREEDOM, THANKS TO LOVE AND FORGIVENESS: STATELESSNESS IN THE DOMINICAN REPUBLIC AND MARK 2:1-12

FRANKELLY MARTÍNEZ

When he returned to Capernaum after some days, it was reported that he was at home. ² So many gathered around that there was no longer room for them, not even in front of the door; and he was speaking the word to them. ³ Then some people came, bringing to him a paralyzed man, carried by four of them. ⁴ And when they could not bring him to Jesus because of the crowd, they removed the roof above him; and after having dug through it, they let down the mat on which the paralytic lay. ⁵ When Jesus saw their faith, he said to the paralytic, "Son, your sins are forgiven." ⁶ Now some of the scribes were sitting there, questioning in their hearts, ⁷ "Why does this fellow speak in this way? It is blasphemy! Who can forgive sins but God alone?" ⁸ At once Jesus perceived in his spirit that they were discussing these questions among themselves; and he said to them, "Why do you raise such questions in your hearts? ⁹ Which is easier, to say to the paralytic, 'Your sins are forgiven,' or to say, 'Stand up and take your mat and walk'? ¹⁰ But so that you may know that the Son of Man has authority on earth to forgive sins"—he said to the paralytic— ¹¹ "I say to you, stand up, take your mat and go to your home." ¹² And he stood up, and

immediately took the mat and went out before all of them; so that they were
all amazed and glorified God, saying, "We have never seen anything like this!"
(Mark 2:1-12)

When I think of a Bible passage really applicable to stateless persons or those in risk of statelessness in the Dominican Republic, I think of this passage. Some call it "Jesus heals a paralytic." Others simply call it "Jesus and the paralytic." Others call it "Sins definitely forgiven." Others call it "Jesus helps a man to walk." We could also entitle it "The hope of the one who walked," or "The blindness of the hearts of stone." We could also call it "The solidarity of four friends." Those titles, obviously, narrow down our understanding of the passage. They place limits on our understanding. However, when we turn to the New Testament in its original Greek, we see that the gospels do not have those sub-headings. Those sub-headings have been a teaching device to help us understand the life given us by the gospels.

Similarly to this text, there is the situation of statelessness or risk of statelessness of hundreds of Dominican men and women of Haitian ancestry and their families. Also, by our so describing them, are we not placing limits on our understanding of that phenomenon, that situation? By describing them as "Dominicans of Haitian ancestry" we are questioning the importance they have, or could have, in the Dominican community, and possibly unleashing prejudices in Dominican society, as also in other human groups that are, or have been, confronted with this issue.

Jesus, healing with authority

I invite you now examine this Bible passage with me. I invite you to examine the lives of those persons, as individuals, as family members, and as members of society. Let us enter into their thinking, their hearts, into the very lives of all those whom we are about to think of. Let us feel what they feel, let us listen to what they are saying, let us look them in the eye. Let us see what journey they are on, what they are doing, whom they are seeing. Let us totally immerse ourselves in the story that we are about to consider.

The words that you will read will be our guide, but this is a journey for you to make, each one of you.

I ask you to pray, reflect slowly and attentively on the passage for this meditation.

> *When he returned to Capernaum after some days, it was reported that he was at home. So many gathered around that there was no longer room for them, not even in front of the door; and he was speaking the word to them. (Mark 2:1-2)*

Jesus had already visited this town. It was there in the synagogue that he had first taught from the scriptures, together with his first close followers, the brothers Simon and Andrew and the brothers James and John. His preaching in that synagogue had been in the form of words and actions by casting out an evil spirit from a man. And he had done it with authority. For that reason, his authority, the people there recognized him. When we are told that he again entered Capernaum, the implication is that Jesus already had a credible reputation in that small town. Capernaum was a little hamlet in the town of Galilee. Its name means "town of Nahum" in honour of the Old Testament prophet of that name. The houses would have been built close to one another, around a large shared courtyard covered with a lightweight roof.

The paralyzed man lying on his mat has not yet arrived. But Jesus is already there before he arrives. Violations, ill treatment, the feeling of powerlessness are never there without Jesus being there already. In the plantation shanty communities, simple clusters like Capernaum, or in places of extreme poverty affecting all those there, Jesus is already there. And the people came after him, another way of describing that they are following him, looking for hope, seeking the good news. Even Satan, the personification of evil, is never there ahead of Jesus, as we see later in Mark's gospel, when Satan, personified in the person of Peter, after Jesus predicts his death, is told, "Get behind me, Satan! You do not have in mind the things of God, but the things of men" (Mark 8:33).

But the good news cannot be silenced, but is scattered to the four winds.

Then some people came, bringing to him a paralyzed man, carried by four of them. (Mark 2:3)

The word had got around that Jesus, the man who had taught with authority (*exousia*), was in the house. And the four men, coming as it were from the four cardinal points, bring their friend who is not able to walk. What sort of a person was this paralyzed man? Was he old, or young? In Galilee, very important everyday tasks were done on foot by walking. So just imagine the powerlessness that this man could have been experiencing at that moment, and indeed his whole life long. In the Acts of the Apostles the followers of Jesus are called followers of the Way. They walked the Way. Way implies the freedom to move. As Paul says in Galatians, it is "for freedom that Christ has set us free" (Gal: 5:1).

Let us imagine our friends who today are not able to obtain an identity document in the Dominican Republic. Like the paralyzed man, they are paralyzed. In the Dominican Republic your identity document gives you the freedom to move around, to walk. For a poor young person, having an identity document means that you are less likely to be apprehended by the police while you are attempting to walk "freely" along the street. Remember, Capernaum is a poor place, where poor people live. In plantation shanties and in the marginalized areas where poor people live, they are even poorer if they are paralyzed, in the sense that they do not have an identity document.

And when they could not bring him to Jesus because of the crowd, they removed the roof above him; and after having dug through it, they let down the mat on which the paralytic lay. When Jesus saw their faith, he said to the paralytic, "Son, your sins are forgiven." (Mark 2:4-5)

The friends realize that it is very difficult to bring the paralyzed man to Jesus, because there was a large crowd. So they opened up the roof to let him down through it. They had great faith, immense faith. Look at the paralyzed man: the text does not say that he could not speak, but that he could not walk. Will the paralyzed man have been talking with his friends? "I want to see Jesus. I want to meet him. I want to speak with him, ask him to help me and tell me what is happening to me. It does not matter what has to be done . . . I want to see his clear eyes, full of goodness, to see my future, and not to be held back by my past, by what I have been, by what I have done wrong, by what my parents probably did wrong. I want him to look at me and begin to speak with me about my future . . . That is what I want. Do whatever it takes, because what I want is for Jesus to see me. We have come a long way, and I want to be with him. And, if I have to come down from the roof, no matter! I can't be any more paralyzed than I already am!"

Dominicans in Haiti

The stateless people in the Dominican Republic have many friends, from various parts of the world, showing their solidarity, their admiration. Some are church members, others are lawyers, others representatives of local and international NGOs, others are leaders and supporters living in the same communities as they do and who understand what is happening in their hearts and lives. They have listened to their description of the situation they are in and have responded to their requests for help. They have presented their case to the international community. They have prayed for them. These friends have come from the four winds, have helped them and are ready to continue bearing their concerns as if they were their own.

Jesus, seeing their faith, the friends' faith and the paralyzed man's faith, forgives him his sins. For many in Jesus' day, the sinful state was the result of actions against God. Some of those sinful actions could be eating without having washed one's hands, going into the temple when unclean, contaminating oneself by worshiping foreign gods. Individuals could also be in a state of sin because their parents had sinned, and they were bearing in their own bodies the consequences of others' actions, and bearing the guilt of it in their own bodies. They were dragging evil along with them. Is that what

God wills – all those individuals bearing on their backs a religious burden of innumerable rules extremely difficult to fulfil, and, moreover, punished and sunk in poverty? Jesus forgives him. Jesus makes him free. He has seen his heart to be full of faith, wishing to meet with God, and Jesus, with the forgiveness, is saying to him, indeed is also saying to his friends, "You have hearts of flesh (Ez. 11:19). You are free, you are forgiven."

Dominicans of Haitian ancestry have been struggling for more than 30 years for their right to have their Dominican nationality recognized. Absurd legal interpretations have been used, so that they have to bear a legal burden too heavy to be borne, laws that basically have been enacted to be applied to this particular group. They suffer from a past of negotiations by the Haitian and Dominican governments, which, during the United States occupation at the beginning of the 20th century (1915–1933 in Haiti and 1916–1924 in the Dominican Republic) began to move the workforce from one location to another in return for payment. That was the beginning of the sugar industry and the beginning of the plantation settlements, one of the places of the greatest concentration of poverty in the whole of the Western hemisphere. Since that date until the 1980s, sugar plantation workers left Haiti to work in the Dominican Republic by means of legal agreements. Many used to remain in the Dominican Republic, while others would return to Haiti. Some of those who remained had families and their children were able to obtain Dominican nationality. Others, however, because of the level of poverty and the weakness of the Dominican civil registration system, never succeeded in obtaining identity documents, nor did their children, nor their children's children. And this lack of identity documents has been passed on from generation to generation. Although all this is in the past, those who had identity documents, as well as those who did not, had the right to Dominican nationality as stipulated in the Dominican Constitution. They suffer from a past of discrimination because of poverty, because the plantation settlements have been isolated for many years with no communication, no basic services and no electricity – all because the prevailing economic model from the second half of the 19th century considers that the only important people are those who have economic resources. They are suffering from a past of cultural discrimination, as do all their compatriots, where black people are considered of less importance in Dominican society, a tangible vestige of a colonial past marked by slavery and inequality. This structural discrimination became internationally known when, on 23 September 2013, the Constitutional Court reached a decision (168 to 13) that definitively states that all individuals born in the Dominican Republic from 1929 to the present day are not Dominican if their parents were in an irregular migratory situation. Like the paralyzed man, this legal historical burden placed on them is breaking their backs and making it impossible for them to move freely.

Jesus and the teachers of the law

Just imagine that we are like the paralyzed man. Just imagine that we are Dominicans of Haitian ancestry. Just imagine how this colonial past bears heavily on the present. Just imagine that Jesus is looking at us with his clear eyes full of life and hope, saying, "You are free. No burden of the past, no legal absurdity, no discrimination is holding you down. I forgive you. You are free."

> *Now some of the scribes were sitting there, questioning in their hearts, "Why does this fellow speak in this way? It is blasphemy! Who can forgive sins but God alone?"(Mark 2:6)*

In Jesus day, more than two thousand years ago, the teachers of the law were responsible for interpreting what God was saying and incorporating it into laws for the people to obey. In the passage that we are examining, we can see that they were sitting, as opposed to the paralyzed man, who was lying on his mat. In the Bible to be sitting shows that the person seated is in a position of power over all the others.

In this fresh scenario, and with the words spoken by Jesus, it would seem from the text that the crowd, the friends, and even the paralyzed man himself fall into the background. It seems that they are not there and the text concentrates on the dispute between Jesus and the teachers of the law. An internal dispute arises, and it would seem that only the teachers of the law and Jesus are visible. Jesus sees in the faces of the teachers of the law what they are thinking in their hearts. Today we speak much of body language and how we communicate more with our body, our gestures, our eyes. Jesus had seen that their attention had strayed from the paralyzed man to Jesus himself. "Who can forgive sins but God alone?" For them, Jesus was blaspheming, and blasphemy was punishable by death.

The same thing has happened in the Dominican Republic. The only ones who can interpret and determine who is, or who is not, Dominican have been the upholders of the legal system. They forget the Constitution and instead fall back on the intricacies of the legal framework. Whoever gives a different interpretation is an enemy of the fatherland, is blaspheming, and is no friend of ours. They forget that the fatherland is the medium used by God and liberty in order to build the Dominican Republic. That is what the Dominican coat of arms says ("Dios, Patria, Libertad" or "God, Fatherland, Liberty"). They have concentrated on the law and forgotten the people. Similarly to those seated teachers of the law, they are feeling that their authority is being threatened. The teachers of the law had forgotten the paralyzed man, but Jesus again turns his attention to the individual.

At once Jesus perceived in his spirit that they were discussing these questions among themselves; and he said to them, "Why do you raise such questions in your hearts? Which is easier, to say to the paralytic, 'Your sins are forgiven,' or to say, 'Stand up and take your mat and walk'? But so that you may know that the Son of Man has authority on earth to forgive sins"—he said to the paralytic—"I say to you, stand up, take your mat and go to your home." And he stood up, and immediately took the mat and went out before all of them; so that they were all amazed and glorified God, saying, "We have never seen anything like this!" (Mark 2:8-12)

Jesus' words are powerful, direct, leaving no room for ambiguity. Jesus was interpreting their body language, and not one of the teachers of the law questions his interpretation. And Jesus asks – and it is not a rhetorical question – "Which is easier to say to the paralytic, 'Your sins are forgiven,'" or to say, 'Stand up and take your mat and walk'?" There is nothing rhetorical about that, for the paralyzed man had been attached for years to his mat, which had "tied him to his sin." And now, he has been freed from "his" sin. So Jesus tells him to take all his past, pick it up, take responsibility for it and go on his way, freely, walking in full view of everyone. People are amazed and begin to recognize that this visible sign, walking, is a sign of what is invisible, his freedom, his release from sin, his being forgiven.

The text does not say at this stage whether the teachers of the law also went away amazed, although we could suspect that their authority was beginning to ebb away with those words and actions of the Son of Man. Later in the gospel, after Jesus had overturned the moneychangers' tables in the Jerusalem temple, we read "priests and the scribes . . . kept looking for a way to kill him" (Mark 11:18).

If we look with the eyes of faith on the situation of the poorest and most impoverished people, and if we look at them as Jesus is now seeing them, the words that he would be saying would be words like these: "Go, continue on your way. There is nothing, or nobody, who can hold you back if you know that I am with you; your rights are guaranteed in this country, or in whatever country you may be living in. Here you are Dominicans. What I desire for you, and for everyone, even for those who are denying you your rights, is life in its fullness, with the possibility to walk in freedom, with food, with the possibility for you and your children to be able to study what your heart desires, with decent work, with the opportunity to live at peace in your community and with the other communities with whom you have relationships. My desire for you, and for everyone, is that you be part of this kingdom of God that is being set up here on earth. What is important for each person is that each individual, and in this case Dominicans of Haitian ancestry, should know this truth in their hearts so that they can walk in freedom. Truth is not located in the legal structures, nor in the structural discrimination of which, in one way or another, we are all part.

The coat of arms of the Dominican Republic has a phrase that must also be understood from the context of the language of John's gospel, and also from this context of exclusion – of the paralyzed man, of the stateless persons in the Dominican Republic, and of the whole world. The interpretation of these words encourages us to move on to actions of love – toward Dominicans of Haitian ancestry, toward the world's poorest, to all: "And you will know the truth, and the truth will make you free" (John 8:32). Truth is in love and love is located more in actions than in words. Love opens doors, doors into the future, because the future, a decent life, freedom, is what makes us human. The kingdom of God is for everyone everywhere – that is the truth that makes us free.

CHAPTER 8

PARTICIPATING IN GOD'S PILGRIMAGE OF JUSTICE AND PEACE: MATT. 10:34-42

FERNANDO ENNS

"Do not think that I have come to bring peace to the earth; I have not come to bring peace, but a sword.

35 For I have come to set a man against his father,
and a daughter against her mother,
and a daughter-in-law against her mother-in-law;
36 and one's foes will be members of one's own household.

37 Whoever loves father or mother more than me is not worthy of me; and whoever loves son or daughter more than me is not worthy of me; 38 and whoever does not take up the cross and follow me is not worthy of me. 39 Those who find their life will lose it, and those who lose their life for my sake will find it.

40 "Whoever welcomes you welcomes me, and whoever welcomes me welcomes the one who sent me. 41 Whoever welcomes a prophet in the name of a prophet will receive a prophet's reward; and whoever welcomes a righteous person in the name of a righteous person will receive the reward of the righteous; 42 and whoever gives even a cup of cold water to one of these little ones in the name of a disciple—truly I tell you, none of these will lose their reward."(Matt. 10:34-42)

The streams of refugees seem to never end: It's becoming desperate. It's quite unpleasant to listen the news these days: in January 2016 there were

60,000 – or was it 80,000? – and that was in Germany alone. Where will we end up – the refugees, this country, Europe? Who could have imagined that we would reach these limits with our open "Schengen-borders"? Who would have thought that after borderless global trade, the boundless flow of finances, and the limitless communication through the World Wide Web the misery of refugees would also be globalized? Terror breaks new ground in Europa: new fences are quickly set up in places where, only 25 years ago, walls were brought down through candles, prayers, and non-violent protests. "We are the people" has suddenly become a slogan of those whose fears make them easy prey for demagogues and hate-mongers.

Every day we see our political systems become more helpless as the right of asylum is gradually denigrated. "Deportation, as soon as possible!" "Send money to Turkey so that the refugees are not let through." "Declare countries safe, so that refugees can be sent back" – potentially including to Afghanistan. "Suspend family reunification!" Surely, there cannot be an "upper limit" on fundamental human rights – that would be the surrendering of our value system in the EU, the utter overturning of our constitutional state. But when will "the mood of the people" decisively shift, the self-fulfilling prophecy that the media has been summoning for months? It is a day to be feared.

Suddenly I realize how this broad public discussion has changed in perspective: it no longer appears to concern the fleeing people, but constantly refers to *us*: *our* society, *our* values, *our* borders, *our* capacity, *our* future. Yet I force myself again to look into those faces: a young man who fled Somalia, whose family raised funds for him so that he could seek a future somewhere else for all of them. Now he is stuck in some "camp" in Serbia. Or the two sisters who fled without their husbands from Afghanistan, but with their small children, and somehow came upon the "Balkan route." Or the Syrian father who could not hold his children on the boat that capsized in the Mediterranean Sea and now returns to fight with the so-called "Islamic State" – against the whole world. And I'm trying to understand, to comprehend, and to perceive what that I cannot grasp.

Biblical orientation for the pilgrimage

How can we – my congregation in Hamburg (Germany), my Mennonite church, the churches in Europe even – continue "on the way"? The World Council of Churches (WCC) in its last assembly in Busan 2013 called for a Pilgrimage of Justice and Peace. This is meant to guide the programmatic work and dedication of the entire WCC for the coming years. For Mennonites, this is a great encouragement, because in this joint decision by Orthodox, Anglican, Lutheran, Reformed, Methodist, Baptist, and many other churches from around the world we recognize that justice and peace are obviously central, not only for our faith as a Peace Church. Together with over 500 million other Christians we are on a Pilgrimage of Justice and Peace, and we call on all people of good will to join us. This is also a truly global undertaking, for which even Pope Francis has expressed appreciation; and the World Evangelical Alliance has signalled willingness to join this pilgrimage. Jews and Muslims are already collaborating in some of our ecumenical working groups around the joint pilgrimage. I feel greatly encouraged by this boundless readiness among such different believers to remain "on the way" together for peace and justice. I am delighted and full of anticipation as to what all may result.

On the other hand, I, as a representative of our small minority tradition of Peace Churches, have also learned from the past to ask critically whether we all mean the same thing when speaking of a Pilgrimage of Justice and Peace. If so many people seem to simply connect in this way, is it perhaps no more than a catchy title under which people can follow their own path? Is it simply a new metaphor to use in running the global "ecumenical circus"?

Let us search for wisdom through the Bible again – just as we have done in discussions of the international WCC reference group for the pilgrimage, which continued its work in Jerusalem last February. I am choosing Jesus' speech to his disciples in Matthew 10 for this missionary discourse to help orient us on the way.

First, the people Jesus commissions are not perfect. All twelve are called by their names, but with character descriptions that could easily be overlooked (Matt. 10:2-4): "the sons of Zebedee" who strive so much to be the greatest; Matthew, "the tax collector"; Thomas, whom we know as the doubter; and Judas Iscariot, "the one who betrayed him." Yes, I can easily see myself in this crowd. The people who are sent here on a pilgrimage are not saints, but the sorts of characters we find in our own congregations, as well as in the other churches. Obviously, perfection is not a precondition to being sent out on this journey.

"As you go, proclaim the good news, 'The kingdom of heaven has come near'" (Matt. 10:7) – So this is their mission: to announce this good news; not at home to themselves, remaining among peers in their own congregations, but to hand out this blessing. In Jesus God became human, and with this movement of God, here is what is certain: the coming of the kingdom of God – meaning what God wants this world be – has already begun. And you are already participating in it. The most wonderful and simple definition of this kingdom of God comes from Paul: "For the kingdom of God is not food and drink but *righteousness* and *peace* and *joy* in the Holy Spirit" (Rom. 14:17). Our Pilgrimage of Justice and Peace is the responsive participation in that kingdom of God, participation in the peace and justice that God has prepared as gifts along the way. "You received without payment; give without payment" (Matt. 10:8). Who would not rejoice? Who would not wish to joyfully participate in this pilgrimage? "Everyone therefore who acknowledges me before others, I also will acknowledge before my Father in heaven," Jesus says to his disciples (Matt. 10:32).

And yet, there is also the other side: "I am sending you out like sheep into the midst of wolves," Jesus warns (Matt. 10:16). This pilgrimage will not be a nice little walk: " Beware of them, for they will hand you over to councils and flog you in their synagogues" (10:17). We know something about this from our Anabaptist-Mennonite history. People who interpreted this kingdom of God, participating in God's justice and peace through a life of nonviolence and conscientious objection to military action, were quickly reviled as "irresponsible enemies of the state." Even today, conscientious objectors in South Korea end up in jail – 800 every year – among criminals. And people who want to live this justice by sharing everything with each other uproot the social and economic order. Even today, small farmers in El Garzál in Colombia are fighting for their right to own their land, and are threatened by the paramilitaries of the landowner, are persecuted, some even killed. The government looks away. "Do not think that I have come to bring peace to the earth; I have not come to bring peace, but a sword"(10:34). And perhaps the most vexing words of Jesus: "And you will be hated by all because of my name" (10:22). Jesus is not deceiving his disciples at all, telling them,"whoever does not take up the cross and follow me is not worthy of me" (10:38).

Suddenly this pilgrimage seems to unfold like a crossroads in front of our eyes: so radical, so brutal. Yet, it is precisely here that it is full of promise: "Those who find their life will lose it, and those who lose their life for my sake will find it" (Matt. 10:39) "When they hand you over, do not worry about how you are to speak or what you are to say; for what you are to say will be given to you at that time; for it is not you who speak, but the Spirit of your Father speaking through you" (10:19-20). The conscientious objectors in South Korea and the small farmers in El Garzál tell me that they only started to understood the truth of these words when they set their feet on the path: "Do not fear those who kill the body but cannot kill the soul" (10:28). They have clung to this promise on their way. And they have realized how little they need on their path of justice and peace: "Take no gold, or silver, or copper in your belts, no bag for your journey, or two tunics, or sandals, or a staff" (10: 9-10) – none of this matters on the way.

Is Jesus' speech, therefore, suggesting that *I* am to go the right way, that *I* am saving my soul, will justify *myself* before *my* God? Of course not! God is not only "my God" but always also the God of the *other*! Jesus does not send his disciples on a trip of self-discovery. He endows them with "authority over unclean spirits, to cast them out, and to cure every disease and every sickness" (Matt. 10:1). He gives them the strength to "cure the sick, raise the dead, cleanse the lepers, cast out demons" (10:8).

That is what this path is all about: the other. The sick. The broken. Those who are held captive by the evil spirits of violence. Those who are driven by the spirits of greed and envy. All of them should be also liberated from the burden of fear that overtakes them because of their wealth; they must be free from the tempting idea that a person must sometimes use force to achieve a little bit of peace; free from the weakness of their own body, because God wants to bear it; free from the fear of their own death, because it blinds them to the great gift of life – life that is salvaged by God, even in and through death. This is the kingdom of God, which began in Jesus because God placed himself on the path, a pilgrimage of justice and peace–– in this life of Jesus – for us.

By this, we should – nay, *we are able* now – to participate in the peace and justice of God´s kingdom and gently walk with God. No one goes alone. Not even the disciples. We shall go on a pilgrimage together, with as many as possible, and in ever-increasing numbers. With those who, inasmuch as we can be liberated from all that (even material) ballast, will be liberated from all worry over what will become of *us*, and also liberated from the hubris that we ourselves could save this world through force and violence. How does that work? Namely, we – like Christ – must turn to the other and thus become "healed healers," as Dorothee Soelle once suggested.

Who is the pilgrim? Whose blessing?

This then could become the new ecumenical Pilgrimage of Justice and Peace, if we learn to understand this pilgrimage in the light of Matthew's gospel. Do others in all the different churches and cultures also understand it in this way? We will only be able to discover the answer if we go with them on this ecumenical path. Already I am starting to dream of what could happen on this common journey, until I'm confronted again by the faces of refugees – in the news, in my city, in my congregation. They're on the go as well, not because they want to, but because they had no other option. Escape, borders, Mediterranean Sea, death, deportation: Theirs is not a "pilgrimage of justice and peace"!

Could it be one, though? Is it totally unthinkable that their refuge might also become a pilgrimage of justice and peace? I hardly dare think along that line, let alone say it out loud. Only here, finally, I discover the last three verses of this missionary discourse of Jesus in the gospel of Matthew:

> *Whoever welcomes you welcomes me, and whoever welcomes me welcomes the one who sent me. Whoever welcomes a prophet in the name of a prophet will receive a prophet's reward; and whoever welcomes a righteous person in the name of a righteous person will receive the reward of the righteous; and whoever gives even a cup of cold water to one of these little ones in the name of a disciple – truly I tell you, none of these will lose their reward. (10:40-42)*

What if this gospel is now, once again prompting us to a change of perspective? Thus far the issue has been those who were sent, and suddenly now it's about those who remain at home. Suddenly the issue is how the disciples are to be taken in, by those who are to be healed, who are to be liberated. Suddenly the issue is how the "pilgrims of justice and peace" are to be welcomed by those who so desperately need healing. Suddenly the issue is how the "least" are received, the "little ones," by those who think so greatly of themselves. If we, who have a home, give them to drink even a cup of cold water – the very least you need to survive on a desert journey to escape terror and death – then we partake of this reality of God's kingdom of peace and justice, and joy! And whoever received the least of these, the little ones, receives Jesus, and, yes, in this way is receiving God himself.

This reading of the passage would indeed change everything, again. In this interpretation, then, would the refugees, the stateless, become the ambassadors of God's kingdom? It would be *them* bringing the kingdom of God at hand, because God wants to meet us *in them*? Would we only then learn from *them* what peace and justice can mean, because we would realize by practising hospitality that we ourselves are the recipients, the ones enriched, and blessed? If that is the case, then the scope of our joint resolution in Busan to begin a global, ecumenical Pilgrimage of Justice and Peace would be revealed to us first and foremost through those "least," the "little ones." Indeed, this is a "mission from the margins" as the new ecumenical understanding of mission phrases it.

A pastor in Hamburg recently said, "I think we still do not realize what a blessing we have actually received through taking in refugees." Maybe we ourselves do not have to embark upon far away pilgrimages to find peace and justice. Perhaps this pilgrimage of God will come right into our own houses, to liberate us *for* peace and justice. The least I will do now is to prepare the cup of cold water. It could well be that God wants to take up residence with me.

—Translated by Jonathan Seiling.

CHAPTER 9

THE FINAL JUDGMENT: REFLECTION ON MATT. 25:31-46

EMMANUEL CLAPSIS

"When the Son of Man comes in his glory, and all the angels with him, then he will sit on the throne of his glory. [32] All the nations will be gathered before him, and he will separate people one from another as a shepherd separates the sheep from the goats, [33] and he will put the sheep at his right hand and the goats at the left. [34] Then the king will say to those at his right hand, 'Come, you that are blessed by my Father, inherit the kingdom prepared for you from the foundation of the world; [35] for I was hungry and you gave me food, I was thirsty and you gave me something to drink, I was a stranger and you welcomed me, [36] I was naked and you gave me clothing, I was sick and you took care of me, I was in prison and you visited me.' [37] Then the righteous will answer him, 'Lord, when was it that we saw you hungry and gave you food, or thirsty and gave you something to drink? [38] And when was it that we saw you a stranger and welcomed you, or naked and gave you clothing? [39] And when was it that we saw you sick or in prison and visited you?' [40] And the king will answer them, 'Truly I tell you, just as you did it to one of the least of these who are members of my family, you did it to me.' [41] Then he will say to those at his left hand, 'You that are accursed, depart from me into the eternal fire prepared for the devil and his angels; [42] for I was hungry and you gave me no food, I was thirsty and you gave me nothing to drink, [43] I was a stranger and you did not welcome

me, naked and you did not give me clothing, sick and in prison and you did not visit me.' [44] *Then they also will answer, 'Lord, when was it that we saw you hungry or thirsty or a stranger or naked or sick or in prison, and did not take care of you?'* [45] *Then he will answer them, 'Truly I tell you, just as you did not do it to one of the least of these, you did not do it to me.'* [46] *And these will go away into eternal punishment, but the righteous into eternal life."(Matt. 25:31-46).*

God's judgment, our choices

The portrayal of the last judgment in Matthew 25:31-46 is one of those classic texts that has inspired and challenged generations of Christians. It has been called the "summary of the gospel"[1] and is one of the most widely cited biblical passages across confessional and religious boundaries. It is the highlight of a discourse in the gospel of Matthew (chapters 24-25) about the signs of the end of history and the coming of the exalted Messiah (24: 3). In 24:4-28 Matthew begins with an account of the last events before the end of history with the appearance of false Christs (24:4-5), wars, natural disasters, persecution, and the fall of Jerusalem. It is apparent, here, that concern is expressed that a believer at the end of times can be deceived about revelation (24:25-27). Following the tribulations of the last days of history comes the cosmic signs and the glorious return of the Son of Man (24:29-31).

For Matthew, the end of times is imminent. It will come within the lifetime of Jesus' (or Matthew's) generation (24:32-35). "All these things" (24:34) will occur within this generation referring to the last historical events (24:8), the cosmic signs (24:32), and the *parousia* itself (24:32-33). But then in 24:36-51 imminence is reinterpreted as uncertainty or unexpectedness. The point now is no longer that the Son of Man will come at a time close to the time of the author of the text but that he may come at a time close to the time of any reader. This shift of emphasis is illustrated in

---

1. «Le sommaire de l'evangile, c'est Matthieu 25/31 a 46» (R. Mehl, «La catholicité de l'église. Commentaire des declarations de l'Assemblée oecuménique d'Upsal,» *Revue d'Histoire et de Philosophie Religieuses* 48 (1968), 369.

the parable of the Wise and Foolish Maidens (25:1-13), which urges vigilance and preparedness for the end of history: Watch, for you do not know the day or the hour. Matthew does not reinterpret imminence as uncertainty by clearly renouncing the former for the latter. He rather leaves them both in the text and only hints that the former is to be seen as the latter. But imminence is still there as itself, alongside uncertainty.

The judgment of God's people as well as of the nations is foretold in both the Hebrew Bible and the New Testament. In particular, the gospel of Matthew does not provide a unified scenario for the final judgment, but rather multiple images. In 13:41, 49 the angels effect the separation of the good and the bad; in 16:27 and 25:31 they passively witness the judgment; in 24:31 they gather the elect from the four corners of the earth. The picture of who will judge is also diverse. In 19:28 the Twelve will sit on the twelve thrones judging the twelve tribes of Israel; in 25:31 the Son of Man alone will judge. Equally problematic is who will be judged. In the interpretation of the parable of the Wheat and the Tares, the angels will gather out of the kingdom "all causes of sin and all evildoers" (13:41), who by implication are members of the community; in the interpretation of the Net the angels will separate simply the "evil from the righteous" (13:49); in 16:27 every person will be judged; in 19:28 the tribes of Israel, and in 24:30 all the tribes of the earth. The language of judgment is powerfully evocative rather than literally descriptive, so that any attempt to define precisely who is meant by different groups in the parable of the Sheep and Goats, as well as in other places (such as the interpretation of the Weeds and the Wheat or the Net), may exact more than the genre permits. The people of God through their belief in God's judgment are reminded what one must do in history to be saved, to have the quality of life that endures. The faithful people by remembering the imminent judgment of God are pressured to make the right choices because there may not be another opportunity to redirect the trend which their choices establishes.

In Matthew 25:31ff the judgment is performed by the Son of Man, who is identified with Jesus of Nazareth, the messianic shepherd and king

(Matt. 25:32, 34), the Son of the Father (25:34) and exalted Lord (25:37, 44), the eschatological Judge. The Judge's identification with a shepherd comes from the Hebrew Bible: God is a shepherd (Ps. 23). The nations, which are to be judged, are separated into the sheep who are put on the right and the goats whose place is on the left. It was natural to choose sheep as the image of the blessed since sheep are whiter and were more valuable commercially, and the Old Testament and the Near East were familiar with the distinction between right and left as positive and negative.

Who's who in the judgment scene?

But who are the nations? Joachim Jeremias holds that the Sheep and the Goats present Matthew's understanding of the salvation of those gentiles who have not heard the message of the gospel. While "the company of disciples" will be judged on the basis of open confession of Jesus (Matt. 10:32), on obedience (7:21), on readiness to forgive (6:14-15), on merciful love (5:7), and on faithful endurance (24:13-14), the gentiles will be justified by works of charity done toward their needy neighbor.[2] Günther Bornkamm[3] thinks that Matthew regards the unbelieving world as being judged along with the disciples, but there is no distinction between the two because both are judged by the same standard of love toward the humblest. While it is true that in Matthew as in the New Testament generally, *ethnos* generally means "gentile" in contrast to Jews, in certain important places the phrase *"panta ta ethne"* must embrace all peoples: "all the nations" is clearly synonymous with the inhabited world. Thus, it is not a term for religious or ethnic divisions (pagan vs. Jew, or pagan vs. Christian).

Who are Jesus' least brothers with whom he identifies himself in this pericope? The expression "my least brothers" combines two terms that Matthew uses for disciples. The disciples are referred to as Jesus' brothers (12:48-50; 28:10), and church members are called "little ones" (18:6,

---

2. Joachim Jeremias, *The Parables of Jesus*, tr. S. H. Hooke (rev. ed.; N.Y.: Charles Scribner's Sons, 1972), 209-10.

3. "End-Expectations and Church in Matthew," *Tradition and Interpretation in Matthew* (Philadelphia: Westminster, 1963), 23-26.

10, 14). Jesus' disciples are his brothers in Matthew, but we learn from 25:31-46 that he has brothers who are not disciples, at least in the understanding of the sheep that served them. This is evident by the surprise when they heard the judgment of the Son of Man. From the standpoint of the sheep's self-understanding, they were not responding to the oppressed because they (oppressed) were disciples of Jesus or because they made Jesus present, but because they were human beings in need. That is why they inherited eternal life.

In the gospel of Matthew, the Son of God / Son of Man not only proclaims the imminent coming of God's reign through his teachings, miracles, and his sacrificial death, but he also communicates the love of God anonymously through his identification with the poor, hungry, and imprisoned. Since both groups know what works of charity are demanded, their surprise comes in the answer of the King that he was identified with the least, who were aided or neglected by those assembled. The primary thrust of the text is the disclosure of the King/Son of Man as hidden in the least, rather than an exhortation to the specific works of charity or even the identification of the least.

The nondisciples and the goats

Non-disciples are responsible to the norm of love, not because all human beings as human beings have been given an effective primordial revelation, but because the Son of Man is present in the poor. But the fact remains that the blessed are not aware that they have met the Son of Man. They are only aware of having performed the acts of care for whomever. Nor did they know until the final judgment that they were to be rewarded; they were not conscious of having served the one who could reward or punish them. They have acted without calculating any benefits at all for themselves.

What about the wondering response of the goats, who are consigned to eternal damnation? Their response to the accusation of the Son of Man can be understood at least in two different ways. The question (when did we see you and not minister to you?) could be taken as the direct refutation of the condemnatory judgment of the Son of God / Son of Man by affirming that they did minister to him. But he replies that in not ministering to his brothers and sisters they did not minister to him. They had assumed, as is evident by their question, that they have done their religious requirements and duties. The goats, according to this line of interpretation, are like the false prophets of 7:21-23, who have confessed Jesus as Lord and have prophesied and worked miracles but have not thereby done the will of God. They are claiming to have done the religious thing and are assuming that that is all which is required.

Another way to understand the question of the goats to the Son of Man is the allusion that they did not see him so how could they have ministered to him? The answer of the Son of Man, in this case, is: You did see me when you saw my brothers, but you did not know what you saw. In this reading, the goats are not so much claiming to have fulfilled the religious requirement as claiming that they have not yet had the obligation or opportunity to fulfil it. When did we ever see anything that would call on us for a response? Evidently the goats had calculated that they had done enough because they are surprised to discover that they have been excluded.

The demands of a loving God

The portrait of the final judgment in the gospel of Matthew is not historiography of a future event, the end of the world. It is rather a parabolic apocalyptic discourse that can be properly interpreted in the greater context of the totality of the biblical revelation. The God of Jesus Christ is, first and always, the Father, who seeks out the lost, not an unmerciful judge whose only satisfaction is to damn. In the biblical discourses of the judgment, what is communicated in the strongest possible manner is what God expects from those with whom he has established a covenantal relationship. It is an invitation to his people to make a decision that brings them closer to God and grants them salvation. They are called to be faithful to God's will as it is disclosed in the history of Israel and, most especially, in the teachings and life pattern of Jesus Christ.

Jesus Christ, in his teaching ministry, juxtaposes the demand of loving God with all one's heart (Deut. 6:5) with the command to love one's neighbour as oneself (Lev. 19:18). By placing these two commands in immediate juxtaposition, Jesus asks us to understand each in light of the other. This is a consistent trend throughout the gospels and even St Paul, as he writes to the Galatians: "Through love become slaves to one another. For the whole law is summed up in a single commandment, "You shall love your neighbor as yourself" (Gal. 5:13-14). The ways we love our neighbour reveal the authenticity of our faith in God in the most concrete terms (1 John 3:16-18).

In the story of the last judgment, the Son of Man, the King, the exalted Lord is identified with the hungry, the thirsty, the strangers, the naked, the sick, and the prisoners of all times and all nations. He bestows the ultimate dignity upon the destitute and marginal by giving himself to them and being unreservedly identified with them. "Truly I tell you, just as you did it to one of the least of these who are members of my family, you did it to me" (Matt. 25:40). In word and deed, Jesus takes to himself, in a very particular way, the ill and the sinners, the despised and the abandoned, and treats them as his equals, making their cause his own. So too he says now that whatever was done to the helpless was done to him. The righteous people certainly did not do this, especially since all people of all times are the judge. If God's love, even his love in Christ, embraces all human beings, then every human being who responds to this love is somehow close to God although he or she may not have been able for multiple different reasons to relate to God through faith in Jesus Christ and conscious participation in the life of his church.

Faith demands an active love toward the poor and the needy (James 2:15-17).

St Gregory of Nyssa exhorts Christians to recognize the true identity of the poor and acknowledge their special dignity.

Do not despise these men in their abjection; do not think them of no account. Reflect what they are and you will understand their dignity; they have taken upon them the person of our Savior. For him, the compassionate, has lent them his person wherewith to abash the unmerciful and the haters of the poor.[4]

The poor, for St John Chrysostom, are liturgical images of the holiest elements in all of the Christian worship: the altar and the body of Christ. "Do you wish to see his altar? . . . This altar is composed of the very members of Christ, and the body of the Lord becomes your altar . . . venerable because it is itself Christ's body . . . This altar you can see lying everywhere, in the alleys and the agoras, and you can sacrifice upon it anytime . . . invoke the spirit not with words, but with deeds.[5] To those who desire to pay homage to Christ, he gives the following advice:

Do you wish to pay homage to Christ's body? Then do not neglect him when he is naked. At the same time that you honor him here [in the church] with hangings made of silk, do not ignore him outside when he perishes from cold and nakedness. For the One who said "This is my body" . . . also said, "When I was hungry you gave me nothing to eat." . . . Your brother is more truly his temple than any church building.[6]

The underlying theological assumption of active concern for those who are suffering is the belief that all people created by God constitute an inextricable unity, and that salvation depends on how we relate to the suffering brethren.

Solidarity and compassion are virtues that all Christians should practise, regardless of their material resources, as signs of their Christian discipleship. The final universal judgment and its reception in the early Christian traditions seem to suggest that charitable action, sympathy for one's fellow man,

---

4. *Love of the Poor*; Walter Shewring, *Rich and Poor in Christian Tradition* (London: Burns, Oates, & Washbourne, 1948), 65.

5. *Epistulam 2 ad Corinthios, Homilia* 20:3.

6. *On Matthew; Homily* 50:4.

is the sole essence of Christianity. Is Christianity simply humanitarianism? There is no doubt that, according to the New Testament, humanitarian conduct is an essential condition of the gospel. But the commandment of love is a new commandment (John 13:34) because it has its basis and possibility in the revelation of God's love for all human beings in Christ.

Living in communion with God is sustained, nourished, and actualized in the church by hearing and proclaiming God's word, the celebration of the holy eucharist, and a life of active compassion and care toward the poor and needy. The churches have given primary emphasis in their lives to one of these three equally important and inseparable ways of being with God (liturgy, scripture, serving the poor). They consider one of them to be more important in constituting their identity, without dismissing the importance of the other two and their inextricable relation with one another. These three modes of being with God cannot be separated without compromising the catholicity of the Christian faith. Scripture, liturgy, and serving the poor are three equally important and inseparable ways of being with God and living in his presence. Whenever one of these is not adequately acknowledged and cultivated together with the other two, the life and the witness, but also the unity, of the Christian church suffers.

Caring for the poor, the needy, the elderly, the homeless, the marginal and abandoned people with no identity and protection is a sacramental act that unites us with God since he has been identified with them and demands that we serve him with acts of justice, compassion, and care. He is with them as he is in the liturgy, and in the proclamation of the Christian gospel.

CHAPTER 10

THE SYROPHOENICIAN WOMAN AND THE ROHINGYA: CALLING FOR GOD'S GRACE

ELENIE POULOS

24 From there he set out and went away to the region of Tyre. He entered a house and did not want anyone to know he was there. Yet he could not escape notice, 25 but a woman whose little daughter had an unclean spirit immediately heard about him, and she came and bowed down at his feet. 26 Now the woman was a Gentile, of Syrophoenician origin. She begged him to cast the demon out of her daughter. 27 He said to her, "Let the children be fed first, for it is not fair to take the children's food and throw it to the dogs." 28 But she answered him, "Sir, even the dogs under the table eat the children's crumbs." 29 Then he said to her, "For saying that, you may go—the demon has left your daughter." 30 So she went home, found the child lying on the bed, and the demon gone. (Mark 7:24-30)

The text in Mark's gospel

Reading Mark's gospel quickly in one sitting, you could be forgiven for thinking that you are reading a Hollywood script for a fast-paced extreme action-horror movie. The action hardly stops. By the end of chapter 1, we have been introduced to one of the most eccentric characters ever described in literature (even ignoring his clothing and the diet, John the Baptist was a bizarre figure); Jesus is baptised in a dramatic scene where the heavens open, the Spirit flies down like a bird, and the voice of God is heard to proclaim his "son-ship"; and in the space of just two verses he is driven into the wilderness to face temptation by Satan, be with "the wild beasts," and receive the care of angels. Then we read of the beginning of Jesus' public ministry, and how with one command he convinces a group of people he'd never met before to leave their lives and follow him to where they knew not.

Then Mark describes a series of miracle healings and exorcisms and relates stories about Jesus behaving badly – mixing with all the wrong people, paying scant regard to the rules of his religion, seeming to deny his family, and telling weird and impossible-to-understand stories about the kingdom of God to confused disciples. If that wasn't enough, there's a storm being stilled, more demons being cast out of a person and into a herd of pigs which then hurl themselves off a cliff, and a dead girl being brought back to life.

The action slows then, just a little – Jesus gets rejected in his home town, sends his disciples off to do their thing, telling them they can't take anything with them, and finally, just before the feeding of the five thousand men and who knows how many women and children, the extraordinary story of the execution of John the Baptist, with his head served up on a platter at a party for the rich and powerful. The day after the feeding of the 5000, Jesus walks on water and continues to heal the countless sick. Then, at the beginning of chapter 7, Mark's Jesus has to deal with his critics—the scribes and the Pharisees (well-educated, pious religious leaders and lawmakers)—on the attack because Jesus is unconcerned by his disciples breaking the purity code.

It is after this that Jesus travels to the northwest, to Tyre, across the Syrian border from the region that was home to him. And it is here, far away from his home that Mark sets yet another story of scandalous behaviour in the encounter between the Palestinian Jew and the gentile woman.

The story of the Syrophoenician woman

The woman who is not named was probably culturally Greek and ethnically Syrian, a foreigner to Jesus: from a different land, different in religion, first language, and culture. She was a woman. She should have been at home and not out on her own, without a man. Jesus was a poor traveller, but she was probably socially elite and wealthy. She was "unclean" or "impure" because of her daughter's illness. Jesus was a religious teacher, not one who should have been in contact with those who would pass on their impurities. She should not have approached him at all, let alone enter a private house and fall to her knees in front of him. Everything about the woman and her actions was an affront to how things should have been. It's no wonder Jesus responded the way he did.

This story is one of the most powerful in the gospels. It appears also in Matthew (where she is referred to as a Canaanite, which still locates her in the Syrophoenician region). It's also one of the most challenging – confronting us with the image of a harsh and dismissive Jesus. Isn't Jesus the one who reaches out to those in need, to those on the margins, those who are vulnerable? But not here, not straight up.

It's curious that Jesus' first response to this woman was to turn her away. The command to care for the stranger (or "alien" as it's often translated) occurs many times in the Hebrew scriptures that Jesus knew so well. There are also many warnings about the consequences for failing to do so. In Leviticus 19 we read: "When an alien resides with you in your land, you shall not oppress the alien. The alien who resides with you shall be to you as the citizen among you; you shall love the alien as yourself, for you were aliens in the land of Egypt: I am the Lord your God" (Lev. 19:33-34). And in Deuteronomy, a warning: "Cursed be anyone who deprives the alien, the orphan, and the widow of justice." (Deut. 27:19a). Throughout the Hebrew scriptures, God is named as the one who cares for the exiled, the one who shelters those most in need, as we read in the prophet Isaiah – God is a shelter from the storm – a shelter from the storms of persecution, marginalization, poverty, and exile.

So why, when confronted with a begging mother, willing to risk everything to save her daughter, did Jesus dismiss her so harshly and cruelly? He compared her to a dog. He was there to feed the children of Israel and she was not one of them. His gifts of grace, his practice of God's hospitality of love, were *not* for outsiders, not for the dogs.

But there was no retreat for this woman who sought healing and inclusion for her beloved daughter. She stood her ground and forced Jesus to engage with her. As human beings, she and her daughter had a right to the grace of God as much as anyone else, even if it was just the scraps of that grace. In the face of this great truth, Jesus changed his mind.

In verse 29, Jesus said, "For saying that, you may go – the demon has left your daughter." The Greek word translated as "saying" is *logos*, the word we associate more often with the "word of God," the "gospel," Jesus' speaking of the good news. But here, the speech that has the power to transform came from the foreigner, the excluded one, and was the word heard by Jesus. The woman brought the word of God, the *logos*, to Jesus; and as the word of God is wont to do, both she and Jesus, and her daughter, were transformed by the encounter.

This story forms a pair with the following one in verses 31-37. In keeping with Mark's fast-paced narrative, one verse after his encounter with the Syrophoenician woman he is far on the other side of Galilee, east, in the Greek region of Decapolis. Here he encounters a man who was deaf, brought to him by others for healing. And again, it is a scandalous story – Jesus breached the purity code by using his own saliva and touching the man, an "unclean" gentile, in order to heal him.

In the context of Mark's story, Jesus' ministry was never the same after these encounters. Until this moment, Jesus' ministry was to Israel alone, but from this point in the gospel, the kingdom of God becomes a gift of grace for all people.

One example will serve to illustrate the "before and after" effect of these stories. In chapter 6, Mark gives us one of the great hospitality stories – the feeding of the five thousand men and uncounted women and children in

Galilee, a Jewish place and a Jewish crowd. In chapter 8, after Jesus' encounters with the two gentiles, Mark offers another miracle feeding – the feeding of the four thousand set in Decapolis, a cosmopolitan place and gentile crowd, where a generosity born of Jewish faith became a miracle of hospitality for everyone.

The text and the case of the Rohingya

It may seem curious to be reflecting on the issue of statelessness through the lens of a text where the main character is identified through nationality or at least "place," but in Mark's gospel this story is one of a number that speaks to Jesus' construction of a "new social order," as Ched Myers describes it. The stories "illustrate the ideology of inclusion, which is the cornerstone to the new social order being constructed by Jesus. The social dynamics of status and honour, fundamental in the life of antiquity, have been turned upside down to make way for the outcast Jew and the alien gentile."[1]

As long as there have been human communities, there have been traditions, practices, and rules – social, political, economic, and religious – that define groups of people against each other: who is "in" and who is "out." In the Palestinian world of Jesus, status in society was formally assigned to people by virtue of their gender and their class, and affected by the Levitical purity code. The purity code further determined inclusion and exclusion from community by virtue of such characteristics as physical disability, demon possession (probably what we understand today as mental health), the menstrual cycle of women, and obedience to the religious rituals that allowed for purification of the temporarily "impure." People were also defined by the place of their birth, their language, culture, and religion.

The Syrophoenician woman reminds us that sometimes it takes more than a little courage to stand up and force the "insiders" to see and acknowledge the right of the "outsiders" to be included. Two thousand years later we are still defining groups of people against each other and identifying people as insiders and outsiders according to certain characteristics. People who are

---

1. Ched Myers, *Binding the Strong Man* (Maryknoll, N.Y.: Orbis Books,1988), 205.

without nationality – stateless – are some of the most invisible outsiders in the world.

I live in Australia, one of the most secure, stable, and prosperous countries in the world, notwithstanding the fact that our indigenous peoples are the most disadvantaged among indigenous peoples anywhere in the world. Australians do not know very much about statelessness. We have a robust, if at times mediocre, democracy. We are far from most of the rest of the world, but every now and again the world breaks in and we glimpse a situation that shocks us. Such was the case in May 2015 when Australians awoke to the story of about eight thousand Rohingya refugees stranded in the Andaman Sea between Bangladesh and Malaysia.

Rohingya people are a Muslim minority from Rakhine State (also known as Arakan) in Myanmar (Burma). Rakhine State borders Bangladesh. Rohingya have lived in Myanmar for centuries. In 1982, the government of Myanmar passed a law to strip Rohingya of their citizenship. The government believes it has no responsibility or duty of care for them because they are Bangladeshi not Burmese. The government now only refers to them as "Bengali." The Rohingya are now stateless and endure state-sanctioned discrimination that includes restrictions on freedom of movement, limited access to education and public services, arbitrary confiscation of property, and even inequitable marriage regulations. Statelessness and this extreme legislative discrimination denying them their basic human rights have combined with brutal persecution by Buddhist extremists to devastate the Rohingya people and drive them from their home. Rohingya are one of the most severely persecuted groups of people in the world.

UNHCR estimates that there more than 800,000 stateless Rohingya in Myanmar. In 2012 alone, about 140,000 people fled their homes, an estimated 86,000 to neighbouring countries.[2] There are at least 200,000 but could be as many as 500,000 Rohingya living in Bangladesh in conditions

---

2. UNHCR, *UNHCR Country Operations profile – Myanmar*, 2015, http://www.unhcr. org/pages/49e4877d6.html; *Refugee Council of Australia, Understanding and Responding to the Rohingya Crisis*, May 2015, http://www.refugeecouncil.org.au/wp-content/ uploads/2015/05/150525-Rohingya.pdf.

that are commonly regarded as the worst for any group of refugees anywhere.[3] It is not surprising that so many choose to flee. UNHCR estimates
that between 2012 and 2015, more than 150,000 people (Rohingya fleeing Myanmar and Bangladesh and Bangladeshis escaping destitution) have
taken to boats to cross the Andaman Sea and the Bay of Bengal. Many of
them have died.

In May 2015, as many as 8000 Rohingya and Bangladeshi people were
stranded at sea. Thailand towed boats back to sea, Malaysia and Indonesia
turned them away and Australia would not help. People were starving. They
had no water. Some died. By the end of May, after significant international
pressure, Indonesia and Malaysia agreed to take in people from any boats
that arrived, on the condition that they would be resettled elsewhere in one
year. Both countries asked the Australian government (a signatory to Refugee Convention, unlike Malaysia and Indonesia) to take some refugees but
the Australian Prime Minister at the time, Tony Abbott said, "Nope, nope,
nope" because "if you want to start a new life, you come through the front
door, not through the back door" and the government did not want to "do
anything that will encourage people to get on boats."[4]

Australia has shut the door to people seeking asylum who arrive by
boat, with policies that include turning back boats, mandatory and indefi-
nite detention in harsh and remote centres in Nauru and Manus Island in
Papua New Guinea, and temporary protection visas with no access to family reunion. Australians are used to harsh speech about refugees and people
seeking asylum, but this off-handed callous response deeply disturbed and
ashamed many people. It reminded me of Jesus' initial response to the
Syrophoenician woman – that she was not one of the chosen ones, not
one of the included, and therefore did not have access to the healing grace
of God.

---

3. Refugee Council of Australia.

4. Lisa Cox,"'Nope, nope, nope': Tony Abbott says Australia Will Not Resettle Refugees in
Migrant Crisis," *Sydney Morning Herald*, 21 May 2015, http://www.smh.com.au/federal-
politics/political-news/nope-nope-nope-tony-abbott-says-australia-will-not-resettle-refu-
gees-in-migrant-crisis-20150521-gh6eew.html.

Statelessness makes people invisible and Rohingya are some of the most invisible people in the world – they are denied the right to live anywhere and denied the right to live with dignity. They are deliberately excluded, forced to live as outsiders, with no state taking responsibility for them. The place of our birth, our language, culture and religion are important aspects of who we are as individuals and communities. The diversity of human life is a gift from God that is to be celebrated and reflects the very nature of God's being. The persecution and exclusion of people because of their culture, language, religion, or ethnicity is, therefore, a sin against God.

Christians have a special responsibility to act against statelessness. The interaction between the Syrophoenician woman and Jesus in Mark's story reminds us that we are all children of God, loved by God, and that together we are the one family of God. There are no outsiders in the household of God. God's will for humankind is that, regardless of how we structure and order our societies, we must live together in peace and with justice.

As Christians, we are called to follow the example of Jesus, who heard and responded to the Syrophoenician woman's argument for access to dignity and who demonstrated a radical inclusive love for all who were excluded, marginalized, and persecuted. We are called to see the people who are invisible, whom others ignore and exclude. We are to hear their stories and speak out against the injustice done to them when they are denied a voice.

The Syrophoenician woman did not give up because she loved her daughter and she knew that God's grace was for everyone. She spoke the word of God to Jesus and it transformed him and possibly even his ministry. We too are called to speak the word of God so that the world will be transformed and all may know the eternal love of God. And we must not ever give up until God's will for a reconciled world is done.

Questions for Reflection and Ideas for Discussion

1. What groups of people are invisible in your society? Why? How do they live?

2. How would your life change if you suddenly lost your citizenship?

3. What does your church do to speak out against racism and religious persecution?

4. Does your church challenge your government when they make bad laws that harm people? Why? Why not?

5. Are the doors of your church building open to those who are on the edges of your society? What does it look like? What would it look like if they were?

Prayer

Loving God,
help us to be true:
to see the truth of our brokenness,
hear the truth of our pain,
and speak the truth of our violence,
regardless of the cost.
Loving God,
help us to be merciful:
to open our hearts to everyone we meet,
to reach out our hands with compassion,
and offer love without condition.
Loving God,
help us to be just:
to transform our violent world –
overturning the systems and structures of oppression
and bringing justice to all creation.
Loving God,
help us to be community:
to live together in trust –
all people and all creation,
reconciled and renewed in your grace,
a world of peace.
Now and forever. Amen

A STATELESS CHURCH CARING FOR STATELESS PEOPLE: A CONTEXTUAL MIDDLE-EASTERN BIBLE STUDY

DANIEL AYUCH

8:1 And Saul approved of their killing him. That day a severe persecution began against the church in Jerusalem, and all except the apostles were scattered throughout the countryside of Judea and Samaria. ² Devout men buried Stephen and made loud lamentation over him. ³ But Saul was ravaging the church by entering house after house; dragging off both men and women, he committed them to prison. ⁴ Now those who were scattered went from place to place, proclaiming the word.

11:19 Now those who were scattered because of the persecution that took place over Stephen traveled as far as Phoenicia, Cyprus, and Antioch, and they spoke the word to no one except Jews. ²⁰ But among them were some men of Cyprus and Cyrene who, on coming to Antioch, spoke to the Hellenists also, proclaiming the Lord Jesus. ²¹ The hand of the Lord was with them, and a great number became believers and turned to the Lord. (Acts 8:1-4 and 11:19-21)

This reading shows the displacement of the first Christian community in Jerusalem triggered by the power of persecution and oppression. The Luke-Acts Diptych gives a long written account of people displacing from city to city and from one region to another. In the gospel, Luke focuses on the Master's continuous movement within Galilee and then towards Jerusalem to finally ascend to heaven. The second volume starts in Jerusalem and it is exactly in 8:1-4, the first paragraph of our reading, where the movement of descending the roads of Jerusalem starts to spread the community everywhere in the inhabited world, until Paul reaches Rome, the capital of the Roman Empire.

One might think that the apostle Paul, a main character of Acts, had it easy with his Roman citizenship (Acts 22:25-29), something similar to the most cosmopolitan passports nowadays. However, one may wonder whether it was really easy for Paul to be citizen of a state that was a persecutor of the community of faith to which he belonged. Luke was aware of the situation of the local communities and their relation to Paul and to the state. But not only Paul was a Roman citizen. Many Christian Jews that lived in diaspora cities had it too, along with some Christians of Gentile origins that were born in free cities of the empire. Other Jewish or Gentile Christians didn't have this distinction and had to flee with less important identity papers that must have caused serious difficulties at the entrances to new cities and at harbors and checkpoints.

The text in its context

At the end of Stephen's sequence, which culminates the Jerusalem cycle in Acts (3:1-8:3), Luke narrates the violent persecution suffered by the believers in the city of Jerusalem and in the surrounding region. Saul's role grows rapidly from eyewitness (7:58) to the one who approves the killing (8:1), and then as the fierce persecutor of Christians (8:3). However, at the end of Acts, Paul will finally take the role of the most persecuted one who is led to Rome to wait for his capital punishment in front of the authorities of his fellow citizens. In his letters, St Paul speaks with rudeness about himself when he remembers how he used to persecute the church (1 Cor. 15:9; Gal. 1:13-23; Phil 3:6). During the golden time of the Jerusalem church, Christians used to pray together in the temple and in houses. This period has been broken and now the time of persecution and abandoning the city has come. But these temporary sufferings are in favor of spreading the word and for the sake of saving many human souls.

The scattering of the community
There is a particular verb that occurs in both paragraphs, in verses 8:4 and 11:19, and draws the reader's attention. It is the Greek verb *diaspeirô* that usually is translated as to scatter although it stems from the simple verb *speirô* which means to sow seeds on a field. With the addition of *"dia-"* the verb takes the sense of sowing seeds *all over* the field, something that in Greek can also mean all over the earth, since the term *gê* means both field and earth.

With this information it is possible to understand the text with a new positive nuance. The disciples were not *scattering* in the negative sense of separating the members of a local church and so exposing the community to be lost, but rather it meant to seed them in new fields in order to spread the Word among new communities. This is also why the communities of Jews outside Palestine were called the Jewish Diaspora, another word that derives from *diaspeirô* having the intrinsic sense of a sowing done by the Lord in a new land. According to Luke, Christ spoke with the disciples before ascending to heaven and gave them the task to be his "witnesses in Jerusalem, in all Judea and Samaria, and to the end of the earth" (Acts 1:8). In our reading Luke says that all believers, except the Apostles, are leaving Jerusalem after six chapters of founding a church in the city and that they are "scattered throughout the countryside of Judea and Samaria" (8:1). No doubt that the persecuting power of the establishment in Jerusalem is now collaborating to fulfil the task given by the resurrected Lord. The apostles stay in Jerusalem for the time being giving to the city the reference value that it has always had. But this is also going to change with Paul's missionary journeys and Peter's departure from Jerusalem: "When morning came, there was no small commotion among the soldiers over what had become of Peter . . . Then he went down from Judea to Caesarea and stayed there" (Acts 12:18s). Acts 8:4

confirms the positive sense of scattering, since *those who were scattered went from place to place, proclaiming the word.* There is no obstacle able to prevent the sowing of the kingdom's seeds. An enraged Saul is described in verse 8:3, who leads the attack operations against Christians. However, nothing can stop the enthusiasm and the force of the believers who trust unconditionally in the Word of God.

Unceasing preaching of the *kerygma*

Between the two parts of our reading, namely between 8:4 and 11:19, Luke narrates the preaching of Philip and Peter and the conversion of Paul on the road to Damascus. Philip preaches in Samaria and Peter in Cesarea while visiting Lydda and Joppa, among other communities. The church has solid communities in different towns while her preachers and missionaries travel around. The reader of Acts does not stay in one place but moves continuously with the preachers from one region to another, from one culture to another and discovers the fortunes and misfortunes of preachers and local churches.

In verse 11:19 the narrator recalls Stephen's martyrdom interlinking both texts before the opening of Paul's missionary journeys. In this second part of the reading Luke leaves Palestine and moves further afield towards Phoenicia (Lebanon), Cyprus and Antioch (in today's Southwest Turkey). It is important to remark that the events of Acts 11:19-21 happen simultaneously with those of 8:1-4. While Peter and Philip were in Palestine and Paul in Damascus, these men and women took other roads. They carried with them their Jewish identity and always lodged among Jewish communities with whom they shared the word of God.

Identity and societal context

It is very interesting to notice the use of the word *Hellenists* in 11:20, which differs with its meaning in 6:1. When Luke talks about the conflict among Hellenists and Hebrews in Acts 6:1 both groups are actually Jews but with different cultural backgrounds: some had Greek education, while others were locals with Aramaic instruction. In 11:20 the narrative takes place in the city of Antioch and there the term *Hellenists* refers to the Gentiles that accept the preaching of those Greek-speaking Christian Jews. This phenomenon is well known by expatriates everywhere in the world. For instance, Lebanese expatriates are regarded by their fellow citizens in Lebanon either as Canadian or French as long as they stay in their homeland and once they are back to their residence countries everyone knows them there as the Lebanese fellows. With the necessary changes, the same happened back in the first century in Jerusalem. Jews living in Greek cities were Hellenists when they came in pilgrimage to the Holy City, but back in their towns they were simply known as Jews.

This is important because it shows how identities can be redefined depending on the social context. These pioneer Christians were actually escaping from persecution and death. One can read only this aspect of their reality and think that among them there must have been children, elderly and sick people that needed especial care and that risked their own lives. However, Luke offers his readers a more triumphalist approach to the situation by saying that "the hand of the Lord was with them," meaning that they were not abandoned to misfortune but, on the contrary, they were always under God's benevolent providence. This is how, despite all odds, they were transformed into preachers of the kingdom and "a great number became believers and turned to the Lord." Of course, this is one's own point of view. Every single person decides to see whether the Lord is there helping them daily and each one decides, as well, whether they want to bear witness to these blessings.

The text in our context

The Patriarchate of Antioch, to which I belong, is a living testimony of church unity, despite the wide array of nationalities and cultures of its people. There is an Antiochian identity, which is an identity of practicing faith in daily life and in liturgy, even though the communities are spread in several Middle Eastern countries and in the diaspora countries all over the world.

For the long memory of the church, belonging to a state is as essential and ephemeral as our personal existence on earth is essential and ephemeral. It is essential because it allows the communities to grow and thrive in any given city or land. And it is ephemeral because it can change due to factors that are often beyond the control of the church and individuals. Christians in Antioch have lived under Roman and Byzantine empires, then under Islamic caliphates, and finally as citizens of modern states. These political changes have affected their lives but they have always kept their faith alive throughout the centuries.

When the recently converted Christian Jews of Hellenistic origins were persecuted in Jerusalem, they did not hesitate to move "back" to their Hellenistic-Roman cities and to carry their faith with them. Also the local Jerusalem Jews who accepted the Christian faith were in need of moving within Palestine. Most probably they did not move further away because their identity papers did not allow them to do so, or because they hoped to return to Jerusalem after the turmoil was over.

By reading the text one understands that the minimal necessities of these families in need of escape suddenly from Jerusalem were somehow covered by other people who took care of them on their road and at the new sojourn place. Certainly those men and women had children and sick people and probably even elderly with them. It seems that long ago the sense of solidarity and hospitality was very much alive. Then the question arises if today humanity has become indifferent to people in need. As a matter of fact we tend to believe the opposite. We are proud of our advancements in international agreements, human rights declarations, and charitably oriented NGOs, as well as of our humanitarian relief organizations. However, there are millions of people lost on their exile roads, with children who are dispersed or were born without papers and families that were torn apart. It seems that the lack of personal engagement in the civilized world has caused an extreme degree of societal indifference, leaving all the responsibility to organizations and institutions and forgetting the importance of assisting the neighbour with our own hands and means.

Today, Syrian Christian refugees all over the world are called to be ambassadors of the Antiochian Christian heritage. If they want to, they can sow the seeds of their faith among the communities that receive them. For them the circumstantial and hopefully ephemeral situation of not having the most convenient and appropriate papers to live and thrive in a city is a reason for worries and sorrows. They have been uprooted from their original cities and villages because of war and suffering. This moment can be seen as a moment of "scattering," like a flock of sheep scatters when the wolf attacks them on the meadow, or it can be approached as a moment of expansion of the church, just as those men and women in our biblical reading did, in the sense of being preachers of the word.

With the beginning of the 20th century and also because of the war, the emigration movement out of the traditional Antiochian territories started to be a massive one. Church authorities were very careful about how to call in Arabic the new communities founded in the Antiochian Diaspora. First they were called "the church in the exile" (*al kanisah fi el mahjar*), probably with the intrinsic hope of an eventual return and in order to reassure their belonging to the Patriarchate. Over time, the communities have been organized into parishes, vicariates, and eventually into dioceses, a fact that is reflected in the new term the church leadership started to use with frequency as of the eighties: "the church in expansion" (*al-kanisah fi el intishar*). In Arabic the most common term for diaspora is *shatat*, a word that reflects the negative sense of scattering or dispersion. This term was certainly used as a mistaken literal translation of "the church in the diaspora"(*al-kanisah fi el shatat*), but it has never been accepted by bishops and the synod, exactly because these communities are not a dispersion of the church but rather an expansion and a development of the church.

The Christian faith is a solid identity for all those who bear the burden of statelessness. It gives them a belonging that makes them accepted as integral persons within the communities of faith. Today's refugees and displaced people have the enormous challenge of facing gigantic political changes and burdensome bureaucratic procedures. Among them, those who believe in

Jesus Christ as Lord and Savior have the opportunity to transform their moment of affliction and worries into moments of hope and providence for the future, while those who enjoy stability and security are called to practise hospitality and offer not only food and shelter but voluntary service and charitable love.

Questions for Reflection

1. Why is it important to see the presence of the Lord in moments of distress?

2. What do you think: is it convenient for a church to have a national identity?

3. Do you have refugees in your community? How is their integration taking place?

4. How different is the role of missionaries for refugees in a new land?

5. What would you do if one day you have to leave your country because of oppression and persecution and found yourself in a new land with very few possessions and almost no rights?

Prayer

Lord God Almighty, Lord of hosts,
Protect at all times those who are displaced and outcast
Because of war and religious persecution.
Give them home, shelter and safety
Through your people of faith, who know your goodness and kindness,
Because you said: "Just as you did it to one of the least of these who are members of my family, you did it to me,"
And you called us to serve those who are in need.
Praised be your Name by our lips and our deeds,
Now and ever, and unto ages of ages, Amen.

CHAPTER 12

CHURCHES OF THE STRANGER: COUNTERING EXCLUSION AND STATELESSNESS

SHIRLEY DEWOLF

2:17 So he came and proclaimed peace to you who were far off and peace to those who were near; 18 for through him both of us have access in one Spirit to the Father. 19 So then you are no longer strangers and aliens, but you are citizens with the saints and also members of the household of God, 20 built upon the foundation of the apostles and prophets, with Christ Jesus himself as the cornerstone...

3:14 For this reason I bow my knees before the Father15 from whom every family] in heaven and on earth takes its name. (Eph. 2:17-20; 3:14-15)

All are citizens in God's household

We are considering our calling as Christians to care more practically for people living among us who are stateless or threatened with statelessness because they fall outside the regular channels for obtaining documents that prove their citizenship. We have come to know young Clémentine, who told us of her loss of parents at an early age and her subsequent life of abuse and exploitation and said, "I do not have a nationality... I stay with the abuse because I have no choice, it is the only way to survive... I feel apart from other people, like I am not a human being. I feel empty, I feel alone."

We heard another stateless young woman say, "I just need one person, only one person, to understand me." Clearly for us this is more than just a matter of getting the documentation right, it is a matter of upholding the dignity of every human being as it has been bestowed on all God's children.

Dietrich Bonhoeffer was the young Lutheran pastor whose Christian witness under the oppression of Nazi-ruled Germany left us with a reminder that Christians must view history from below, from the margins, because that is where Jesus stood. From there we a have totally different perspective than from the centre of power. Paul wrote in a similar vein when he told of how Jesus emptied himself of all divine power and privilege and humbled himself to take on the life of a human slave, which gave him the perspective from which he could be totally obedient to God's will. And in that famous passage from Philippians 2, Paul urges us: "Let the same mind be in you" (Phil. 2:5).

From the margins of society, the good news that Jesus came to demonstrate to us is that in the unlimited scope of God's amazing grace – a love that does not focus on our sins but on our needs – every person is a citizen in God's household and every family takes its name, its core identity, from the fatherhood of God. Jesus' sacrifice for our sins on the cross created of us a new humanity where the divisive walls of religion, ethnicity, gender, nationality, and historical generations are simply removed and we belong to each other because we all belong to him. Therein lies our human dignity as individuals and therein lies the dignity of the human race.

That must be the grounding of our plan of action as we find our way forward in our efforts to prevent and cure exclusion and statelessness. If not, we run the risk of simply taking up a project that could divide people further: everyone will have the correct paperwork, but this could feed hostile boundaries and self-centred identity groups that are emerging and undermine God's project of a united and harmonious world. Documentation, important as it is, cannot be the end goal of the church, because it is only one means to reaching that goal. Human dignity within the inclusive family of God must always be our greater vision.

In 1993 there was a very important gathering of African church leaders called together in Nyeri, Kenya. It was not the stature of the people who attended that made the meeting important, nor the number of churches they represented as members of the All Africa Conference of Churches (AACC). Rather, this meeting was important because of a concept that emerged from the floor that grew and clarified the call to mission of many of those of us who were present.

On the first day someone put up a chart on the wall that showed the increase in the number of refugees and internally displaced persons in Africa in the more or less 30 years since the AACC opened its refugee service program. It was a disturbing chart, with a red line that rose sharply and showed clearly the alarming rate at which the people of our continent were being forced out of their homes and communities into hazardous lives and uncertain futures. Then someone called for a graph in green that would show the growth in African church membership over the same period of time. We were shocked when we saw that the red and green lines on the two graphs ascended at an almost parallel rate. Staring us in the face was the fact that while we were rejoicing over the dramatic increase in church membership over the past 30 years, the Christianizing of our continent was having little effect on the causes that pushed our people into untold suffering. Something was clearly wrong with our understanding of the nature and mission of the church in Africa as it related to the dignity of human life.

The next morning our meditation was led by brothers and sisters from the Egyptian churches. They read from Mathew 25, where Jesus said "I was a stranger" and they gave their testimony. Nearly two thousand years ago there was upheaval in Palestine and many people fled to Egypt for refuge. Among them was a young boy-child. We have no documented record of him in the historical annals of our nation. He lived among us for several years, but he went unnoticed. He was invisible, a stranger, one more mouth to feed among the thousands. It was only many years later that we came to know this child as Jesus, our Saviour. So we in Egypt are truly the Church of the Stranger among us.

Their testimony helped us to understand the problem we were facing across Africa: it was an identity problem. We had been the Church of Many Good Works, the Church of Millions of Members, the Church of the Loud Voice. But we had not yet become the Church of the Stranger, the church which today is challenged by the cry of the young girl we heard: "I just need one person, only one person, to understand me." With our membership of millions across the continent, where have we been all her life?

UNHCR has launched a campaign called "I Belong." That is basically a biblical theme. So what would it mean to be a church that not only seeks national belonging for others, but more importantly affirms and extends God's gift of belonging in the familyhood of God? Belonging is a God-given human need and is expressed in community. In community we share name and identity. It means common ownership, where we all take responsibility to ensure each other's well-being. It means each of us has the freedom to contribute from our individual strengths, but also the freedom to be forgiven when we make mistakes. It means having an orderly framework that holds us together. It means shared laughter and tears. Belonging does not mean everyone in the community is the same, but it means we appreciate each other's unique experiences and perspectives as a channel through which God nurtures us all. That is the vision we Christians have for our nations as communities and toward which we are actively urging our governments to build their systems of governance. But let us look closer to home. Can we honestly say that this kind of belonging can be found in our congregations? Are we truly the Church of the Stranger, where no one is a stranger?

The story of Theresa

Let me share with you the story of Theresa. The pastor of one of our congregations in the border town of Mutare first came across Theresa when she was arrested with a group of six hundred migrant workers of various nationalities found working at an illegal gold mining site in Zimbabwe. The Christian Council of Mozambique, who were at the time helping to resettle post-war returnees to their country, picked up the story from the press and contacted the ecumenical forum in Mutare to ask them to look into the matter. When the pastor assigned to the task went to the police station he found our Zimbabwean police in the process of deporting the six hundred through the border post, but thanks to a shortage of police vehicles that was slowing down the process, he found Theresa and her two youngest children still locked up and he had to time to hear her story.

Theresa was born and raised in a small village near Gogoi in Mozambique, close to the Zimbabwe border. At 16 she became pregnant and marriage arrangements were made for her with a neighbour family. Soon after the baby was born, the war in Mozambique reached her village, her parents were killed and Theresa was raped. When she was found to be pregnant, her boyfriend and his family rejected her, not even willing to recognize the child from her first pregnancy. Theresa wandered about in the forest, and by God's mercy she came across a kindly stranger in the forest who sent her to his cousin across the border in Zimbabwe for help. In the Rusitu Valley of Zimbabwe Theresa was given a small field on which to grow maize for herself and two small children, but just before harvest the Zimbabwe police moved in, chased away all the people who could not show Zimbabwean identity papers, and destroyed the maize field. Theresa and her children were forced back into Mozambican territory and, in desperation, she approached a man and offered to become his property in return for her labour in his field. When the war in Mozambique ended, this man decided to return to his original home in the north of the country but would not take Theresa and the children with him. By now she had a third child. Theresa heard of a small gold mine within Zimbabwe where the owner would take on anyone willing to work with no questions about nationality or documentation. So she crossed back into Zimbabwe with her three children and went to find the mine. One of the foremen pays the school fees of her two older children, but in return she had to move into his house along with two other women. A fourth child was born to Theresa from this union.

Then came the mine raid by Zimbabwean police, the arrest of the six hundred illegally operating migrant workers, and the pastor's discovery of

Theresa and her two youngest children in the Mutare jail. I cannot help but wonder in a continent full of Christians why this was the first time anyone from the church took an interest in her. The pastor heard Theresa's story and promised to try and recover her two older children left behind at the mine. He could not prevent the police from deporting her, but a week later she made her way back across the porous border into Mutare and found the pastor. His congregation helped reunite her little family, found her a place to stay, and helped her set up a stall at the marketplace where she could buy and sell tomatoes for a meager income. Theresa became a faithful attendant at the weekly services of their church.

This sounds as though it was a happy ending to a very difficult story, but it was not. Throughout the time she worshiped in that church, Theresa was never fully accepted. She was always considered a stranger, a "public woman" whose series of relationships with men left her suspect and made her children different from other people's children. Theresa could not qualify to join the women's guild and she would never be considered good enough to be elected to a leadership role or represent the congregation at any meetings. She was the object of the church members' pity and they often gave her used items from their homes to help her cope, but she never received their respect. Theresa and her children did not find belonging in that church, they were not extended the liberating good news that they were citizens together with the saints and full members of the grace-filled household of God. May the Lord forgive us for trying to be the Church of the Pure, rather than of the Church of the Stranger!

What would have happened in your congregation – where would Theresa and her children have found themselves? Perhaps you would known better than our pastor how to approach UNHCR or Lawyers for Human Rights to seek help for Theresa in sorting out her citizenship and documentation issues, so that her choices in life would be more secure. But at a social and spiritual level, in your community, would Theresa and her family find the absolute acceptance and the resulting depth of healing that is the unmistakable mark of the grace of God?

As we move forward today with our plans for the church to challenge systems and structures that allow statelessness, let us begin with some self-examination to make sure we are ready for this task. How broad do we think our mandate is: Are we ready to take on the full scope of Jesus' inclusive ministry? Are we prepared to do the most we can rather than the least we can get by with, heeding Jesus' piercing question to his followers: "What more are you doing than others?" Have we assumed that this work is actually UNHCR's or UNICEF's job and we, the church, have been called in to play an auxiliary role? Is this ministry in our hearts: Are we outraged enough when the dignity of people's full personhood is denied, either by the state or by the church? When Theresa and Clémentine look into the face of the church, what do they see? What do we need to empty ourselves of in order to become the Church of Jesus Christ the Stranger?

Whatever it takes to ensure that all people are treated with dignity, let us be determined to ensure that it is done. Thanks be to God for this opportunity to be useful in God's work.